English For The Workplace

ESL for Action

Problem Posing at Work

Elsa Roberts Auerbach
Nina Wallerstein

 Addison-Wesley Publishing Company

Reading, Massachusetts • Menlo Park, California
Don Mills, Ontario • Wokingham, England • Amsterdam • Bonn • Sydney
Singapore • Tokyo • Madrid • Bogota • Santiago • San Juan

Text Credits

pp. 6–7, Manh's Life Journey from *English as a Second Language Resource Manual* by Patsy Price and Shel Montgomery. Edmonton: Alberta Vocational Centre, 1985, p. 245.
p. 8, Cheap Labor in Asia from *Women in the Global Factory* by Annette Fuente and Barbara Ehrenreich. Boston: South End Press, 1983.
pp. 21–23, Information in U.S. Immigration Patterns adapted from *Scholastic Update*, Sept. 6, 1985, p. 6 and Thomas Muller and Thomas Espenshade, *The Fourth Wave: California's Newest Immigrants*. Washington, D.C.: Urban Institute Press, 1985.
p. 25, Code adapted from *Juan Manuel Looks for a Job* by Sheila Bell, Kathleen Jo Tobias, Jean Unda and student writers. Toronto: St. Christopher House/Participatory Research Group.
p. 26, Obstacles chart adapted from *Making Changes: Employment Orientation for Immigrant Women* by May Ann Kainola. Toronto: Cross Cultural Communication Centre, 1982.
p. 38, excerpts from *Working* by Studs Terkel. NY: Avon, 1974.
p. 78, excerpt from *Your Rights on the Job* by Robert Schwartz. Boston: The Labor Guild of Boston, 1983, p. 81.
p. 83, Interview with an Undocumented Worker adapted from "The New Immigrants" in *The Labor Page*, No. 15–16, Summer 1984.
p. 87, Grammar Practice adapted from *Immigrants Speak Out* by dian marino and Deborah Barndt. Toronto Participatory Research Group, 1985.
p. 89, Time Management adapted from *Teaching English in the Workplace*, by M.E. Belfiore and B. Burnaby. Toronto: OISE Press, 1984, p. 107.
p. 95, Voices from History from *Bitter Wages* by J. Page and M.W. O'Brien. NY: Grossman, 1973.

p. 124, Voices from History from *Amoskeag: Life and Work in an American Factory City* by Tamara K. Hareven and Randolph Langenbach. NY: Pantheon Books, 1978, pp. 127, 160.
p. 131, Figure from *Progress*, Fall 1985, Vol. 6, No. 2:1.
p. 133, Hoagie Siebert Reading from *Women and the World of Work* by Azi Ellowitch. Philadelphia: Lutheran Settlement House Women's Program, 1983, p. 34.
p. 137, Interview with Chha Vy by Shirley Mark Yuen in *Progress*, Fall 1985, Vol. 6, No. 2:2.
p. 161, "The Talk is Union, the Tongues are Asian," by Lynda Gorov in *The Boston Globe*, December 11, 1984, p. 33.
p. 170, Reading from *Time Magazine*, July 8, 1985, pp. 37, 49.
pp. 172–3, "Sewing on Their Own," by Jan Gilbrecht excerpted from *Dollars and Sense*, September 1985, pp. 12–14.
pp. 173–4, "Cambodians Protest Job Program" by Henrietta Charles in *Long Beach Press-Telegram*, February 26, 1986.

Photo Credits

pp. 36, 114, Naomi Wall, *We Make the Clothes*. Toronto: Toronto Board of Education, 1985.
p. 159, Cathy Cade
p. 174, Tom Shaw, *Long Beach Press Telegram*, Feb. 26, 1986.

Cartoon Credits

pp. 52, 55, 60, 66, 74, 91, 112, 128, 158, 163 by Fred Wright, *So Long Partner!* NY: United Electrical Radio and Machine Workers of America, 1975.

A Publication of the World Language Division

Project Coordinator: Kathleen Sands-Boehmer
Production/Manufacturing: James W. Gibbons
Design: Al Burkhardt
Illustrations: Mary Burkhardt
Cover Design: Gary Fujiwara
Cover Photo Credits: Ken Light © 1986 and Cathy Cade
Production Service: Jeanine Ardourel & Associates

Legal information from Robert M. Schwartz, *Your Rights on the Job*, Boston: Labor Guild, 1983

ISBN 0-201-00101-2
11 12 13 14 15 16 17 18 19 20 - CRS - 98 97 96 95

Contents

"I have many problems, but my problems help me to learn."

Maria Mete, ESL Student

Preface

This Student Book accompanied by a Teacher's Guide concerns education for change: the personal and social changes that we, as teachers, hope to promote in the lives of our students and in our own lives.

The lessons explore the daily work lives of immigrants, both past and present: their interactions with people from different nationalities, with American co-workers, supervisors, and union representatives; their concerns with health and safety, working conditions, stress, and pay; their vulnerabilities (low expectations, low self-esteem) in American work sites that inhibit language-learning; and, finally, the individual and group actions students need to take to learn English, gain self-confidence, and assert their rights at work.

Both the Student Book and Teacher's Guide together are based on the educational process of dialogue called "problem-posing." Originally developed by Brazilian educator Paulo Freire, problem-posing starts from students' lives and asks them to "believe in themselves ... that they have knowledge."[1] Problem-posing assumes that education is not value-free, but is embedded in a social context. Students bring to the classroom a richness of experience: their culture, their troubles, and their skills. Everyone—teachers and students, administrators and teachers—participates in dialogue as co-learners.

The goal of problem-posing dialogue is critical thinking and action, which starts from perceiving the social, historical, or cultural causes of problems in one's life. But critical thinking continues beyond perception—toward the actions and decisions people take to gain control over their lives. As a group process, problem-posing enables people to see social connections, rather than blame themselves for having difficulty "making it" in America, and to gain self-confidence to act outside the classroom to make changes in their lives.

The first step to promoting action outside the classroom is to transform education inside the classroom. Our role as teachers is to create a safe environment in which students can express opinions and, most importantly, generate their own language materials for learning and peer-teaching. Curriculum is not a *product* (developed before the start of the program), but a *process*, which is constantly created through participant interaction. Because of the social and emotional involvement in curriculum that comes from students' lives, problem-posing becomes a powerful motivating factor in language acquisition. As students learn the methodology, they also begin to assume responsibility for their own learning. By changing traditional classroom roles, students will be able to re-examine their traditional workplace roles.

A problem-posing methodology has three phases: *listening* (or investigating the issues of the community), *dialogue* (or codifying issues into discussion "codes" for critical thinking), and *action* (or strategizing the changes students envision following reflection). Each of these stages is explored in detail in the Teacher's Guide, with many suggested activities for how to listen for critical issues, both in and outside the classroom; how to bring issues into the classroom through creating codes; how to use the problem-posing questioning strategy with codes to elicit dialogue; how to use codes to address the potentially threatening or overwhelming problems that students raise; and how to encourage student actions to challenge the problems in their lives. Actions, both in and outside the classroom, are examined for their role in creating true knowledge based on experience and reflection. Many examples are given to demonstrate the three stages. (See

---

[1] Freire, Paulo, "By Learning They Can Teach," *Convergence*, 6(1):78–84, 1973.

"Using the Book" in the Student Book for a brief description of Codes and Questions for Discussion.)

In one sense, working from a published student text is antithetical to genuine problem-posing; lessons are best generated from stories and issues from members of a particular class. Teaching time constraints and similar workplace issues, however, make a text an appropriate starting place for classroom interaction and student-produced materials. In this spirit of inspiring student "ownership" of their learning, we offer the Student Book as a model of problem-posing for teaching English in worksite settings, i.e., pre-vocational or vocational classes, employee or employer-sponsored programs, community ESL or labor classes. We hope our examples will support teachers and will stimulate curriculum-writing by students.

The Teacher's Guide to this Student Book is critical to fully understand the problem-posing approach and creation of new curriculum. Presenting a general methodology, the Guide will be vital for community and labor educators, teachers and administrators engaged in "education for change" within a broad range of adult education programs: literacy, ESL, worker, health, and health and safety education.

The expanded preface in the Teacher's Guide includes questions you may have as teachers using this approach with some of our responses. Three additional chapters contain in-depth information on problem-posing. Chapter 1: "Teaching Approach" explores the historical background of Freire's literacy program, the philosophy and three-stage problem-posing methodology, the role of the teacher as facilitator, and curriculum evaluation suggestions. Chapter 2: "Meaning of Work" discusses the contribution immigrant workers have made to the building of America and provides information on dilemmas facing immigrant and American workers in today's workplaces. Chapter 3: "Teacher Training" takes educators through a step-by-step workshop on how to create a "problem-posing" program in a community, with examples from ESL/literacy, health, and labor programs in North America. Chapter 4 provides examples from the Health and Safety Unit and a model unit (not included in the Student Book) on loss of work: it treats layoffs, collecting unemployment, quitting, getting fired, plant closings and surviving unemployment. Classes dealing with these issues should refer

to the Teacher's Guide for this student material. An extensive Resources section will help teachers and students to investigate further those themes that apply to their particular situations.

Change—personal, educational, or social—is an ongoing and difficult process. In problem-posing, change starts with education in the classroom, enabling students to gain self-confidence as co-learners and decision-makers. Through language development and action activities, we encourage students to act outside the classroom. In problem-posing, action or following through to the consequences of discussion is essential for learning. Action for students means learning to see themselves as social and political beings, by having a safe classroom environment to test out ideas and by receiving support to apply their opinions and assert their rights outside the classroom in their workplaces and their communities.

But the process of change demands time and continuing commitment. We therefore call our educational approach *problem-posing*, and not problem-solving. We must be "patiently impatient," Paulo Freire tells us, as we painstakingly move toward a better society. Although change may evolve slowly, problem-posing nurtures this process. It is important to explore the problems and their causes, but also the dreams and ideals our students have for themselves, their families, their communities, and their work; we can help them explore these visions as they develop language skills, self-esteem, and competencies to assume control in their lives.

We wrote this book, therefore, to share our belief that learning and participating in change is an exciting and joyful process. There is a growing movement of educators throughout the world engaged in problem-posing. Many of the materials and exercises presented here come from our students, and from teachers in the United States and Canada who have shared their ideas in workshops and in their own writings. We hope to continue this exchange of ideas and would appreciate any comments or thoughts as you and your students try out the lessons in this book and create your own.

Nina Wallerstein
University of New Mexico, Albuquerque

Elsa Auerbach
University of Massachusetts, Boston

January, 1987

Using the Book

The nine units in this book take you through the daily lives and issues of working people: how they get a job, how they relate to co-workers and supervisors, how they face work stresses and health and safety problems, how as minorities and women, workers face special pressures on the job and at home, and how they can participate in activities to improve their work situations. Each unit follows the problem-posing methodology: identifying the issues from work, analyzing the causes of the problems, and developing strategies for change.

Language and competency instruction are integrated throughout each lesson to support the goal of action for change. In the initial code and dialogue sections, the primary language instruction is vocabulary clarification and exchange of students' interpretations of the problem. In the thinking activities that follow, charts, collages, peer interviews, and true stories are used to elicit language patterns from students and to deepen their analysis of the social context of the problem. Finally, the action activities, such as action competencies and research, provide tools for addressing the problems.

The language level of the book is primarily intermediate, though each lesson contains both simpler and more advanced materials. The true stories, for example, are written at a lower level than the historical or legal readings. Teachers may simplify the advanced sections, use them as teacher resources, or for lower level classes present the content in students' first language (with a translator's help).

Each unit represents a major problem area in students' working lives. The units follow an overall sequence, although after the first few, they can be taught in any order, depending on class concerns. If a discussion in class raises an issue covered later, you have a few choices: hold the subject for another day, ask students to write a story or code for immediate or later use, or skip to the unit of interest and work through those lessons. You can always return to the original unit.

A few of the units contain essential lessons for any class. Unit I sets the tone of the entire book, that students' experiences and feelings are integral to learning: students introduce themselves and their life histories, and acknowledge cultural conflicts in learning English. Lesson 3 explicitly addresses different language learning expectations to establish a framework for negotiating differences. Unit II raises students' personal and social roles in the workplace in light of U.S. immigrant labor history. Included is a guide to the reading process used for passages throughout the text. Unit III asks students to describe their daily work and interactions.

Unit IV, Lesson 1, makes explicit the problem-posing process so students can apply it to their own lives. Unit V deepens discussion of working conditions and explores policies expected on the job site. Unit VI raises the vital concern of how to improve health and safety conditions. Unit VII addresses issues of equal treatment for immigrants, minorities, and women. Unit VIII details union procedures and allows students to see how unions and workers can work together for change. Finally, Unit IX emphasizes the need for students to overcome differences with other workers, to find common ground for actions, and to look toward their futures. It invites students to continue to generate their own text as part of the process.

Although you may decide to follow all units in sequence, some lessons may not be applicable to your class. A group of men may prefer to omit the lesson on pregnancy. The unit on unions, however, may be important even if students don't have a union in their current jobs. The key is to start from relevant issues that enable students to analyze and envision a better situation.

Organization of the Lessons

Each unit includes several lessons. Each lesson contains different activities that proceed through the entire problem-posing process, from description, through analysis, to action.

CODES: Lessons start with a code—a physical representation of a critical issue, i.e., a problematic work theme, that has emerged during the listening stage. Usually in the form of a written dialogue, story, or graphic, the code re-presents the students' reality back to them and allows them to project their emotional and social responses in a focused fashion. An effective code should be a familiar situation that presents the many sides of the problem, with *no* solution. The problem should not be overwhelming, but offer possibilities for small actions toward change that affirm and emerge from the group. Codes are more than visual aids, for their purpose is to promote critical thinking and action about the important or loaded issues in people's lives.

Dialogue codes can be acted out by students, cut into strips and reconstructed, or read by the teacher and an advanced student (in classes with uneven literacy skills). After discussion on the code, students can act out the same or similar situations with their own endings.

QUESTIONS FOR DISCUSSION: Although codes present open-ended situations, critical thinking does not occur spontaneously. Problem-posing with a code uses a five-step inductive questioning strategy that directs discussion from the concrete to the analytic level. Students are asked to: 1) describe the situation, 2) identify the problem, 3) relate the problem to their own experience, 4) analyze the underlying social or cultural reasons for the problem, and 5) seek methods for change. As students share experiences in step 3, they begin to see the broader social context to problems. The final questioning step takes students into positive action with strategies or solutions that emerge from the group experience. The questions in the text are meant as *guidelines*, rather than rigid prescriptions; students and teachers will find their own questions as they explore the code.

As the lesson progresses, problem-posing assumes a deeper structural thread. The code and questions for discussion serve primarily for students to identify problems and discuss their personal involvement (steps 1 to 3), though students will also elaborate root causes and possible actions (steps 4 and 5). (See the Teacher's Guide for indepth analysis of codes and questions.)

THINKING ACTIVITIES: The thinking activities that follow the questions for discussion delve deeper into step 4, asking the question, "why?" Thinking activities provide multiple opportunities for students to expand their views and redefine the social parameters of the problem. Students will also begin the process of conceptualizing solutions, which they will put into practice in the action activities section. Different techniques are incorporated into the thinking activities, including vocabulary, grammar practice, role plays, peer interviews, and charts.

CHARTS: Charts are an effective tool to present new information or to sum up the class experience. Students can easily pool their individual experience into a visual representation of the group. For instance, you may ask the class about signs and causes of stress. You can list individual responses in a chart form on the board or on butcher paper. As people literally see how their responses compare with others, they begin to place the issue in a wider social context. Charts also become a basis for grammar practice using student information. The teacher presents the structure and students do pattern drills, substituting their own experience.

GRAMMAR: Grammar teaching is based on content elicited from students through many techniques in the book: charts, communicative exercises, question formation in interviews, practice of modals with open-ended stories ("what should Maria do?"), and specific grammar exercises (see the Appendix).

TRUE STORIES: Often, short open-ended true stories are presented about a worker's problem. The stories contain no solution and students are asked to propose their own. They first think about or write solutions individually and then rank these from best to worst. They compare solutions in small groups and try to arrive at a consensus or group solution. Each small group presents a solution and rationale for the choice to the class.

ACTION ACTIVITIES: Action activities follow thinking activities to give students tools for change, elaborating on step 5 in the questioning sequence. The emphasis on action increases from the middle of the book as students develop self-confidence through the problem-posing process to become more effective actors in their lives. These activities may be listed as action competencies or role plays.

ACTION COMPETENCIES: Action competencies emphasize individual self-confidence, such as asking for help, or group actions, such as reporting a problem to supervisors. They usually offer a model dialogue and its components. Students can generate alternative language forms and practice the competencies through role plays of different situations. (For a list of competencies, see the Appendix.)

ROLE PLAYS: Role plays provide a forum to use new information, practice competencies, and try out other endings for the codes, stories, or competencies. Discussion after the role plays enables students to evaluate critically the implications of the different endings.

READINGS: Legal Readings, Voices from History, and news articles help students identify their choices in the thinking and action activities. The high interest content motivates students to develop reading skills. Students are encouraged to read small sections of texts collaboratively in groups and report on their conclusions to the class. By sharing their information, students become experts on small chunks of material, minimizing the role of teacher as the source of all knowledge. Students may use pre-reading strategies, by building schema, selecting key words, and writing comprehension questions. After each reading, class discussion should relate the material to students' own experiences. (See the Appendix for a list; legal readings are noted by an asterisk.)

STUDENT ACTION RESEARCH: Through research activities, students can practice their classroom learning by investigations outside the classroom. Students research their own work sites through interviews, recorded observations, collection of forms and documents, and contacts with local agencies. As students formulate their own questions and report on the findings, they become experts on their work sites and learn tools for continuing the process. Students gain language skills and confidence to identify alternative workplace actions, make contacts with co-workers, evaluate results, and learn how to approach problems in a positive way.

LOGS: Many lessons end with a log which brings the concept of action back into the classroom. Students write stories or dialogue codes about their research or about issues discussed in class. These are then used for further exploration of the problem. Writing their own curriculum materials gives students a genuine opportunity to "take control" of their education; hopefully they learn they can "take control" of their lives outside the classroom as well.

Acknowledgments

This project is truly the result of a collective effort: much of the inspiration and content grew out of shared experiences at the workplace and in the classroom, from dialogue, laughter, and struggle with co-workers and students. They, as much as we, are the authors of this text.

We especially want to thank our colleagues, fellow teachers, students, friends, and families for their encouragement to write this together, even though we live in opposite corners of the country.

There are many individuals who gave freely and generously of their time and expertise. Bob Schwartz, a labor lawyer and author of *Your Rights on the Job* (Boston: Labor Guild, 1983), carefully reviewed the readings on workers' rights, offering helpful suggestions and corrections. Harvey Kaplan, an immigration lawyer, helped to revise the legal information in the deportation lesson. Jim Green, a labor historian, guided us toward relevant historical literature and opened his bookshelves to us for further research. We owe a special debt of gratitude to Loren McGrail for her early enthusiasm about this project, for testing the materials, and for her thoughtful feedback and support at every stage of the process.

Many of our Canadian friends inspired this project with their pioneering work and generously shared materials with us. In particular, we would like to thank Deborah Barndt, Jean Unda, and Naomi Wall for their direct and indirect assistance.

We owe special thanks to the immigrants and refugees whose stories appear in this volume (many of whom wish to remain anonymous). In particular, we thank Em Truong for his insightful critiques of codes, for the many stories he contributed to the text, and for having the courage to look critically at his world.

We are grateful to all those who allowed us to use their work in the text: to the United Electrical, Radio and Machine Workers (UE) for the use of Fred Wright's cartoons, to the Lutheran Settlement House Women's Program, Women for Economic Justice, the *Labor Page*, the Alberta Vocational Centre, the *Boston Globe*, and many others. We are particularly appreciative of the support of Kathy Sands-Boehmer at Addison-Wesley, who had the unenviable task of challenging us to be concise and molding our dream into marketable form.— **E.R.A.** and **N.W.**

I want especially to thank my colleagues at the University of Massachusetts for their encouragement with this project, Mei-zhu Lui for continuing to struggle and for pushing me to struggle, John Auerbach for anchoring me, valuing my work, and living his principles, and Nicholas and Jessica for their support and patience—**E.R.A.**

I owe special thanks to Edward Bernstein, Suzanne Korey, and Pia Moriarty for many discussions that sharpened my ideas, and to David Dunaway for his constant editorial assistance, support, and patience in the final stages.—**N.W.**

Introducing Ourselves

Lesson 1   Introductions: What's Your Name?

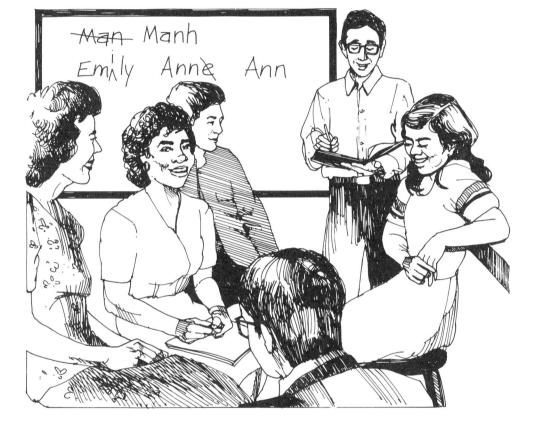

INTRODUCTORY ACTIVITY: Getting started

1. Make a circle with your chairs. Go around the circle and introduce yourselves:

"My name is _____. What's yours?"

2. Tell the teacher one name you remember. He or she will write it on the board:

"This is Mario."

"That is _____."

3. Is everyone's name on the board? Ask each other questions until all the names are written correctly.

CODE

Supervisor: Stella, this is Duc Nguyen. Please show him the job.

American worker: Sure. What's your name again?

Vietnamese worker: Nguyen Duc.

Stella: What was that?

Duc: It's Duc.

Stella: (*laughing*) It sounds like Duck. I guess I'll call you Doug. My name is Stella.

Duc: Tella?

Stella: No! STELLA. S-T-E-L-L-A.

Duc: OK.

Questions for discussion:

1. What is the Vietnamese worker's name?
What does the supervisor call him?
Can Stella say Duc's name?
Can Duc say Stella's name?

2. What does Stella call Duc?
How do you think Duc feels about this?
What does Duc call Stella?
How do you think Stella feels about this?

3. Do Americans ever have trouble with your name?
What do they call you? Do you like it?
Do you have trouble with American names?

4. In your country, are family names first or last?
In your country, who do you call by their first name?
In your country, who do you call by a title (Teacher, Sir, Grandmother, Doctor)?
Do you think immigrants should take English names? Why or why not?

5. What can you say if Americans have trouble with your name?
What can you say if you have trouble with a name?

THINKING ACTIVITIES

A. NAMING SYSTEMS: Getting information

In pairs, find out about each others' names. Ask these questions; ask your teacher, too.

1. What is your name?
2. What is your *family name* (or *last name*)?
3. What is your *first name*?
4. What is your *middle name*?
5. (For married women): What is your *maiden name*?
6. In your country, do you keep your parents' name when you get married?
7. In your country, what do you call your teacher?
8. What do you want to be called?

Discussion: You feel comfortable calling your teacher "Teacher" or
Mr. _____, but he wants to be called by his first name. What should
you do?

B. NAMING SYSTEMS: Chart

Make a class chart of name differences in your countries.

Country	Names
U.S.	First, Middle, Last
China	Last, Middle, First

Grammar Practice (simple present tense—*to be*): Make sentences like these
about your chart:

> In the U.S., the family name is last.   In China, the family name is first.

ACTION ACTIVITIES

A. COMPETENCY: Asking for help with names

What does Stella say when she doesn't understand Duc's name?
What other questions can you ask to get help with names?
Practice asking for help with other students' names.

> Example: Student #1: This is Nicholas.
>   Student #2: I'm sorry. What was that?

B. COMPETENCY: Polite ways to keep your name

Do Americans sometimes change your name? What do they call you? What do
you want to be called? What can you say to keep your name? Add to this list:

> I'd rather be called _____.   I prefer _____.

Practice this conversation, using each others' names:

Stella: What's your name again?
Nguyen Duc: Nguyen Duc. Duc.
Stella: Can I call you Doug?
Duc: I prefer Duc.

C. STUDENT INTERVIEWS

CLASS QUESTIONS: What would you like to know about each other? Make a list of questions to ask each other using *what*, *where*, and *why*. Then ask the questions in pairs.

Examples: *What* country are you from?
What kind of work do you do?

Where do you work?
Where do you live?

Why do you want to learn English?
Why did you come to the U.S.?

INTRODUCTIONS: Introduce your partner to the class.

Example: This is Duc. He is from Vietnam. He works at the Marriott Hotel. He came here because of the war in his country. His brother is here.

CLASS CHART: After you've introduced each other, make a chart about the students in class.

Name	Where are you from?	What do you do?
Duc	Vietnam	Housekeeping/hotel
Hien	Vietnam	No job

Grammar Practice: Make sentences like this:

Duc and Hien are from Vietnam.

CLASS CHART: Make another chart about your class. What is the same about the students? What is different?

Same	Different
all women	countries
no English	jobs

STUDENT ACTION RESEARCH

Ask three friends about name problems:

1. What do Americans call you?
2. What do you want to be called?
3. Do you think immigrants should keep their names or take American names? Why?

Discuss your interviews in class: Why do some people want American names? Why do others *not* want them?

Lesson 2   Life Journeys: Where Are You From?

INTRODUCTORY ACTIVITY: Map

Use a big map of the world. Draw different colored lines to show the paths that
people in your class traveled to come to the United States.

IMMIGRATION CHART

What was happening in your country when you came here? Why did you
choose the U.S.? Put the information on a chart like this one:

NAME	YOUR COUNTRY	UNITED STATES
MANH	WAR	PEACEFUL LIFE
CHIANG	LOW WAGES (NO MONEY)	MORE MONEY
ANNA	DICTATOR	SISTER

Discussion: What are some of the main reasons immigrants and refugees
come to the U.S.?

CODE

Manh's Life Journey

Questions for discussion:

1. Where is Manh from?
 When was he born?
 When did he leave his homeland?
 How did he get to Hong Kong?
 How long did he stay in Hong Kong?
 What did he do there?
 When did he go to Canada? How did he get there?

2. How did he feel about Vietnam?
 Why do you think he left?
 What happened when he left?
 How did he feel about Hong Kong?
 Why do you think he left?
 How does he feel about Canada?

3. Where were you born?
 How long did you live in your country?
 What did you do there?
 Where did you go when you left your country?
 How did you get to the United States?
 How do you feel about your country? About the U.S.?

4. Why do people leave their countries?
 How do people feel when they come to a new country?

5. What can you do to make your life better in a new place?

READING: Manh's life Journey

Here is the story Manh wrote about his life journey:

I traveled to Hong Kong by boat. The Vietnamese airplane shot at our boat, but they missed.

In Hong Kong, I worked in the Miltwright Cookie factory as a cookie maker for 3 years. In 1982–84, I also worked in this factory as a mechanic making the pans and cookie molds.

I arrived in Canada on September 17, 1984. I like Edmonton very much. Also I enjoy learning English to make a new life in Canada.

I like Canada so much; however, I am afraid of the winter in Canada. Sometimes I feel homesick because my parents and my sisters are still living in Vietnam.

I'm very happy now. I think spring is coming. It'll warm up my life, so I won't feel lonely anymore. I'll go fishing with my brothers as soon as possible.

Questions for discussion:

1. What questions do you want to ask about Manh's life?

2. How is your life like Manh's? How is it different?

3. Make up three questions about Manh's story. Ask each other these questions. Don't ask the same question twice.

Grammar Practice (*simple past tense*): Underline all the verbs in Manh's story that talk about something that happened in the past. Do they all have the same endings? Underline the past tense verbs in these questions, then answer the questions *if you want to.* Your teacher will write the past tense verbs from your answers on the board.

1. Where were you born?

2. When were you born?

3. Where did you work or go to school?

4. When did you leave your country?

5. Where did you go when you left?

6. How did you get there?

7. When did you come to the U.S.?

8. Who came with you?

9. Who (in your family) is still home?

10. What was happening in your country when you left?

11. What did you hope for in the U.S.?

12. What did you find in the U.S.?

Make lists of regular and irregular past tense verbs from Manh's story and these questions. Add to your lists as you learn new verbs.

THINKING ACTIVITY: Life Journeys

A. YOUR TEACHER'S LIFE JOURNEY

Ask your teacher to draw a time line of his or her life. Ask questions using *when, where, what, who,* and *why.*

B. YOUR LIFE JOURNEY

Now draw a time line of your life journey on a separate sheet of paper. Share your life journeys in small groups. Ask each other questions like these:

What happened before you _____?

What happened after you _____?

What happened when you _____?

What was happening in your country when you left?

_____?

What is happening in your country now? _____?

C. REASONS FOR COMING HERE

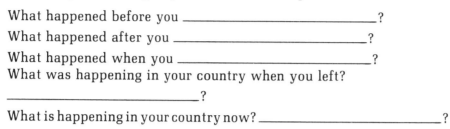

CHEAP LABOR IN ASIA
Hourly Wages in U.S. Dollars

	Wages	Wages and Fringe Benefits
Hong Kong	$1.15	$1.20
Singapore	.79	1.25
South Korea	.63	2.00
Taiwan	.53	.80
Malaysia	.48	.60
Philippines	.48	.50
Indonesia	.19	.35

Source: *Semiconductor International*, February 1982, quoted in *Women in the Global Factory.*

Questions for discussion:

1. How much do these workers make for each hour of work?
2. How much is the minimum wage in the United States?
3. How much do workers make in your country?
4. Is it easy or hard to find jobs in your country?
5. Do you earn more or less in the U.S.?
6. Why do you think many American companies build factories in Asian countries?

STUDENT ACTION RESEARCH

A. EXPERIENCE STORIES

1. *Tell your story:* Bring in a photo of yourself. Tell the story of your life journey into a tape recorder.

2. *Write your story:* Your teacher or other students can write it with you or for you.

3. *Revise your story:* Go over the story with other students. What do they want to know more about? What can you add? What can you leave out? Do you want to correct grammar problems? Do you want to leave the story as it is?

4. *Make a book:* When your story is done, put your picture on it. Make a class book about your life journeys, or make a book about your own life story.

B. DREAM COLLAGES

What did you think about the U.S. before you came? Cut out pictures from newspapers, magazines, and catalogues that show what you expected in the U.S. Glue them on a large piece of paper or file folder. Share them in pairs.

Questions for discussion:

1. What was your dream of America before you came?

2. Where did you get your ideas about the U.S.?

3. What happened when you got here?

4. What is the same as your dream? What is different?

5. What would you tell someone from your country who wanted to come to the U.S.?

6. What can you do to make your life here better?

Lesson 3   English Class: What Did You Say?

INTRODUCTORY ACTIVITY

Where is this woman?

How does she feel?
Is she happy?
     sad?
     worried?
     angry?
     tired?
     scared?
     lost?
     confused?

Why do you think she feels
  this way?

Where are these people?

How do they feel?
Are they happy?
     sad?
     worried?
     angry?
     tired?
     scared?
     lost?
     confused?

Why do you think they feel
  this way?

CODE

Jose: Where are you going?

Maria: To English class. Do you want to come?

Jose: I don't have time. I have two jobs.

Maria: You live in the U.S. now. You need English.

Jose: No, I don't. Everyone at work speaks Portuguese. My friends are
Portuguese and I go to Portuguese stores.

Maria: Don't you want a better job than this?

Jose: I know lots of English-speaking people with no jobs. Anyway, I'll never
learn English. It's too hard. I'm too old.

Questions for discussion:

1. What language are Maria and Jose speaking?
Where is Maria going?
Where is Jose going?
Does Jose want to learn English?

2. How does Maria feel about English?
Why does Jose not want to go to English class?
Why do you think Jose has two jobs?
Does he need English?

3. Do you ever feel like Jose?
Why are you studying English?
When or where do you need English?

4. Do you think Jose or Maria is right? Why?
Do people always need English for work?
What jobs do you need English for?
Will you get a good job if your English is good?

5. What do you want to learn in English class?
What can your teacher teach you?
What can you teach others in English class?
What are some good ways to learn a language?
What do you think should happen in a language classroom?

THINKING ACTIVITIES: Learning English

A. REASONS FOR STUDYING ENGLISH

Each of these students needs English for a different reason:

João: My son calls me stupid, but in Portuguese I am smarter than he is.

Pedro: The Americans get angry when we speak Spanish at work.

Chi-Wei: I want to be a waiter, not a dishwasher.

Maria: I want to help my children with homework.

Why do you need English? Who do you want to talk to? What do you want
to do? Make a chart like this for your class:

Name	Needs to	Wants to
Pierre	talk to his boss	read the paper
Anna	talk to the doctor	help her children

Grammar Practice: Use the chart to make sentences like these:

> Pierre needs to talk to his boss.
> Raoul and Anna want to help their children.

Discussion: What are some common reasons that you need English? List
them on the board.

B. WAYS TO LEARN A LANGUAGE

What do you think students should do in English class? Put a check next to the phrases you agree with. Talk about your answers.

_____ If you're not sure about something, *guess*.

_____ Listen a lot; do not talk much.

_____ Memorize grammar rules.

_____ Ask questions if you don't understand.

_____ Have discussions about work problems.

_____ Do grammar drills.

_____ Do a lot of reading.

_____ Do a lot of writing.

_____ Talk only when the teacher calls on you.

_____ Try to talk even if you might be wrong.

_____ Sit quietly if you don't understand.

_____ Practice language you will need at work.

_____ Be careful not to make mistakes.

_____ Other: What else do you think should happen in English class?
We should _____

GRAMMAR: Adjectives

Each of the students below has strong feelings about English class. How do you think he/she feels? Use the following words to describe each student.

happy	scared	worried	confused	bored
homesick	lost	impatient	interested	angry

1. My teacher talks too fast. I don't understand her. — She feels <u>lost and scared.</u>

2. It's too hard to study after work. I can't stay awake in class. — He feels _____.

3. My class is too easy. I'm not learning anything new. — He _____.

4. I can't pay attention. I'm thinking about my family in Puerto Rico all the time. — She _____.

5. I love my class. I learn something new every day. — She _____.

6. We have to read too much. I can't read English. — She _____.

7. I don't have time to study. I have to take care of my children. — She _____.

8. I'm not learning fast enough. It will take too long to learn. — He _____.

9. My husband doesn't want me to learn English. He is afraid I will be too independent. — She _____.

Which of these sentences talks about how you feel? Draw a picture of yourself in class; write a sentence under it to describe your feelings about class. Make sentences like these about yourself:

1. I feel *sad* when _____.

2. I feel *nervous* when _____.

ACTION ACTIVITIES

A. COMPETENCY: Asking for repetition in class

If you can't understand something in class, what can you say? Add to this list:

> Could you please talk more slowly?
> I'm sorry. I didn't get that.
> Would you mind repeating that?
> I'm sorry. I still don't understand.

Practice: Your teacher will dictate some sentences. If you don't understand, ask for repetition.

B. COMPETENCY: Asking for feedback and correction

What can you say to find out if you're right? Add to the list:

> Did I do this right?
> Is this right?
> Did I spell this right?
> Could you check this?

Write two sentences about your English class. Ask someone for help. Ask someone else to check your work.

C. QUESTION CHART

Make a large chart of questions to help you in English class and put it on the wall.

> Some Questions:
>
> • What does _____ mean?
> • How do you spell _____?
> • Could you repeat that?
> • Could you speak slowly, please?
> • Is this right?
> • (Add your own.)

D. PROBLEMS IN CLASS

Look at these problems. What do you think the student should do? First list all the possibilities. Then choose the best one. Discuss your answers.

1. Maria's teacher talks too fast.

> Example: She can ask the teacher to speak slower.
> She can change to a new class.
> She can quit.
> She can sit quietly and listen.

2. George feels his class is too hard.
3. Anna is always too tired to study after work.
4. Hien thinks his teacher gives too much work. He doesn't have time to do it.
5. Maria thinks the class is too slow.
6. Jesus thinks about his family problems in class and can't pay attention.
7. Hien has to miss class.
8. Em wants to do more writing and less talking in class.
9. I (add your own) _____

E. ROLE PLAY

Divide into groups and choose one problem that students have in English class. Act out what the student could say and how the teacher might respond.

LEARNING TIP: Vocabulary strategy

The authors do not explain every new word in this book. What can you do if you don't understand a word? Look at these suggestions and add your own. Ask your teacher for other ideas. Then check *good* or *not good* next to each.

	good	not good
1. Look it up in the dictionary.	___	___
2. Guess its meaning.	___	___
3. Ask your teacher about every new word.	___	___
4. Try to figure it out from the sentence it's in.	___	___
5. Stop listening.	___	___
6. Ask about important words.	___	___
7. Keep your own list or dictionary of new words.	___	___
8. Skip unimportant words.	___	___
9. _____	___	___

Choose five new words from this lesson and find out what they mean. Begin your own word list.

LOG

Talk about one time when you needed English and you didn't have it. What happened? Your teacher will write some of your stories. You will get copies of the stories to keep. These stories (and others that you write later) will become a textbook that the class can use for future lessons.

EVALUATION

Discuss what you liked in the unit, what you did not like, what you learned, and what you want to learn. After each unit, make an evaluation sheet like this one.

I LIKED:	a lot	so-so	not much
1. Talking about names.	___	___	___
2. Talking about life journeys.	___	___	___
3. Talking about learning English.	___	___	___
4. Making charts.	___	___	___
5. Reading stories about people.	___	___	___
6. Writing stories.	___	___	___
7. Talking about how people feel.	___	___	___
8. Grammar exercises.	___	___	___
9. Learning how to do things (ask for repetition, ask for help).	___	___	___
10. Role plays.	___	___	___
11. Other _____	___	___	___

I CAN:	easily	sometimes	not at all
1. Ask for help with names.	___	___	___
2. Help people with my name.	___	___	___
3. Introduce someone.	___	___	___
4. Talk about my past.	___	___	___
5. Ask for help with spelling.	___	___	___
6. Ask for help with new words.	___	___	___
7. Ask for repetition.	___	___	___
8. Other _____	___	___	___

I WANT TO: Make a list of things you want to work on in English class.

Work with other students to make a class chart.

I NEED TO: Make a list of things you need to work on more.

Getting a Job

Lesson 1   Jobs at Home and Jobs in the U.S.

CODE

Interviewer: Tell me about your work experience.

Le Minh: In my country, I was a college math teacher. I taught math for ten years.

Interviewer: Have you ever worked in a hospital?

Le Minh: No, but I like to work with people.

Interviewer: There is an opening in the kitchen. Are you interested?

Le Minh: I guess so.

Questions for discussion:

1. What did Le Minh do in his country?
 What does the interviewer ask him?
 What job is open?

2. Why do you think the interviewer suggests the kitchen job?
 How do you think Le Minh feels about the kitchen job?
 Is it a good job for Le Minh? Why or why not?

3. What did you do in your country?
 What do you do in the U.S.?
 How do you feel about your job?
 What do you want to do?

4. Did many immigrants come to the U.S. from your country?
 When did they come? Why did they come?
 What kinds of jobs did they do?
 Why do many immigrants and refugees have low-paying jobs?
 Do you think non-Americans have to start at the bottom?
   Why or why not?

5. What can you do to get a better job?

THINKING ACTIVITIES

A. LE MINH'S CHOICES

What do you think Le Minh should do? By yourself, rank his choices from 1 to 5 (best to worst); in small groups, try to agree on the best choice.

____ He should take any job he can get.

____ He should work in the kitchen and go to school at night.

____ He should look for a job in a bilingual math class.

____ He should look for a computer training program.

____ Other: _____

Individual Solution	Group Solution
_____	_____
_____	_____
_____	_____
_____	_____
_____	_____

B. JOBS CHART

Make a class chart like this one:

Name	Jobs at home	Jobs in the U.S.
Le Minh	math teacher	dishwasher
Anh	store owner	cook's helper

C. WHAT'S A GOOD JOB?

What makes a job "good"? What is important for you?

	Important	Not very important
To make a lot of money.	___	___
To have a clean job.	___	___
To help other people.	___	___
To have a lot of education.	___	___
To have good hours.	___	___
To be your own boss.	___	___
To have a safe job.	___	___
To have people respect you.	___	___
To use your head.	___	___
Other _____	___	___

GRAMMAR: Comparative and Superlative Adjectives

A. COMPARATIVES

Ask each other these questions:

hard	Is factory work *harder* than teaching?
safe	Is being a teacher *safer* than being a cashier?
clean	Is housekeeping *cleaner* than farming?
easy	Is childcare *easier* than factory work?
interesting	Is electronics *more interesting* than cooking?
difficult	Is using your head *more difficult* than using your hands?

Look at the italicized words. How are they made?
When do you add -er?
What happens to the -y in *easy* when you add -er?
When do you add the word *more*?

Grammar Practice: Use these words to make comparisons about things you know.

> smart   old   easy   dirty   lazy   strong   fast   cold   hard
> beautiful   afraid   helpful   confused   difficult   friendly

B. SUPERLATIVES

Look at the italicized words below. How are they made?

safe	What was the *safest* place you ever lived?
easy	What was the *easiest* language you ever learned?
interesting	What is the *most interesting* job you ever had?
good	The *best* job I ever had was teaching.
bad	The *worst* job I ever had was cleaning houses.

Grammar Practice: Make your own sentences using superlatives of the words in part A, above.

ACTION ACTIVITIES: Choosing Jobs

When you look for a job, you need to think about your *experience*, your *skills*, your *education*, and your *preferences*.

A. YOUR EXPERIENCE

Your past jobs are your *experience*. Look at these three ways of talking about job experience. How are they the same? How are they different?

1. I was a farmer and a car mechanic at home.
2. I used to be a farmer and a car mechanic in Laos.
3. I worked as a farmer and a car mechanic in my country.

Look at these ways of talking about experience in the U.S.:

1. I worked in a shoe factory in New York. I was a packer.
2. I worked in the Marriott Hotel in Boston. I was a cook.

Grammar Practice: Make sentences about your job experience.

B. YOUR SKILLS

What do you know how to do? What are you good at? These are your *skills*. Make a chart to show all your skills at work and at home.

Jobs in Homeland	First Job in U.S.	Present Job	Home
Store Owner	Janitor	Factory	
talk to customers	sweep, mop	lift	fixing
keep books	wax machine	read codes	cars
make orders	wash windows	sort	plumbing
take money	small repairs	drive forklift	carpentry
supervise help			
pay bills			

Grammar Practice: Make sentences like these about your skills:

> I can keep books.   I can fix cars.
> I like to keep books.   I like to fix cars.
> I'm good at keeping books.   I'm good at fixing cars.

C. YOUR EDUCATION

How many years of school have you had? What kind of schools did you go to? Make a chart like this one to show your *education*:

Dates	Place/Location	School
1986	Boston, Massachusetts	International Institute
1985	Galang, Indonesia	Refugee Camp
1980–83	Saigon, Vietnam	Secondary School

D. YOUR JOB PREFERENCES

What is important for you in a job? What kind of work would you like to do? These are your *preferences*. Ask and answer these questions with a partner.

1. Do you want to work alone or with other people?

> Example: I prefer to work with people.
> *or* I would rather work with people.

2. Do you want to work full-time or part-time?
3. Do you want to work in a small place or a large place?
4. Do you want to work in the day or at night?
5. Do you want to work with your head or with your hands?
6. (Add your own question.) _____

E. PUTTING IT ALL TOGETHER

Write down your experience:

1. Job #1 _____
2. Job #2 _____
3. Job #3 _____

Write down your education:

1. elementary school (years) _____
2. high school (years) _____
3. college/university _____
    major _____
4. special training _____

Write down your skills:	Write down your preferences:
1. _____	**1.** _____
2. _____	**2.** _____
3. _____	**3.** _____

In small groups, look at your lists and discuss three kinds of jobs that might be good for you.

STUDENT ACTION RESEARCH

JOB APPLICATION: Ask a friend to get you a job application from his or her workplace. Fill it out in class with a partner.

INTERVIEWS: Talk to someone who does a job you might like. Ask what he or she does every day. Ask what experience, education, and skills you need for that job. Share your answers in class.

RESUME: Ask your teacher to bring in a resume. What are the main parts of a resume? Make a resume of your own, listing your education, skills, and experience.

READING: Voices from History

Sometimes students think that they need to understand every word of an article. They read carefully, from beginning to end, looking up new words. Often this takes a long time and makes reading more difficult. Here are some ways to make reading easier and quicker:

1. Before you read, look at the title, headings, pictures, charts, and italicized words. Guess what the article is about.
2. What do you already know about this topic? Discuss it as a class. Make up questions about the article.
3. Read the first paragraph and the end of the article first. Often they tell you the author's main point.
4. As you read, DO NOT LOOK UP WORDS. Guess the words. If you stop to look up words, your reading will be slow and you will have a harder time understanding the whole meaning of the article.

With this reading, do these pre-reading exercises as a group:

1. Read just the title and headings; guess what the article will be about.
2. Read the introduction; talk about what you already know about the topic.
3. Make up some questions about the reading.

After you do these exercises as a class, divide into groups. Each group should read one section and report on it to the class. *Follow the same guidelines for all the readings in this book.*

U.S. Immigration Patterns

Introduction: Since 1607, we have accepted two-thirds of the world's immigrants—a total of 50 million people. But U.S. laws designed to restrict immigrants kept out millions of others. Moreover, millions who did settle in the U.S. encountered prejudice and sometimes even violence.[1]

America is a land of immigrants. Yet it has not always welcomed immigrants with open arms. On the one hand, immigration has been encouraged when there was a need for foreign labor; on the other, immigrants have been blamed for political and economic problems here. Patterns of immigration closely follow the needs of the American economy: when there is a need for labor, laws encourage immigration; when there is unemployment and depression, laws restrict immigration.

The Early Years of the Nation: The first immigrants to the U.S. were forced to come here to fill particular labor needs. Slaves were brought from Africa to develop the Southern farm economy. Indentured servants were brought from Scotland and Ireland; recruiters went to Europe to get skilled workers to develop American industry.

However, in 1798 the first laws against immigrants were passed (The Alien and Sedition Acts). The government was afraid that immigrants might bring in revolutionary ideas. These laws said that immigrants must live here for 14 years to become citizens.

The Early 1800s: These mixed feelings towards immigrants have continued ever since. In the early 1800s waves of Irish Catholics came to the U.S. to get away from poverty and famine in Ireland. They became the low wage factory workers that built industrialism in the Northeast.

[1] *Scholastic Update*, September 6, 1985, p. 6.

Bad feelings toward these immigrants flared up after 1830: an anti-immigrant political group, the Know-Nothings, wanted "America for the Americans." They called the Irish drunken, violent and ignorant. Much of this feeling came from a fear of immigrant political power.

The Chinese: In the mid-1800s thousands of Chinese were brought to the West by employers like the Pacific Central Railroad. As a rule, they performed unskilled labor, the kind of strenuous and menial jobs which whites tended to shy away from. As long as they were needed to build the railroads, they were welcomed (always in the low-skilled jobs). However, when the railroads were completed and as the Chinese began to compete with American workers for other jobs, mob violence against the Chinese became common on the West Coast. In 1882, the Chinese Exclusion Act was passed: Chinese workers were excluded from the country and Congress banned most Chinese immigration. This was the first law to limit immigration by nationality. Between 1882 and 1902, the U.S. Congress passed thirteen discriminatory laws against the Chinese, including laws excluding the immigration of Chinese women. The Exclusion Act was law until 1943.

The Turn of the Century: Between 1890 and 1920, there were 18.2 million immigrants to the U.S., mostly from Southern and Eastern Europe. American employers encouraged immigration by giving cheap boat passage and promises of a good life in the U.S. For example, a *padrone* would go to Europe to recruit unskilled labor on contract with a promise of free ship passage and a fixed wage. When they got to the U.S., whole gangs of workers were given to an employer with a profit for the *padrone*.

By 1910, the majority of workers in many industries were immigrants: 70% of the iron miners, 65% of the garment workers, and 50% of the iron and steel workers. "These new immigrants suffered the same sort of discrimination that the Irish had endured earlier. Italians were identified with organized crime . . . Though most likely to be garment workers laboring in sweatshops for miserable wages, Jews were caricatured as moneylenders and international financiers."[2]

Immigrants became active in early trade union organizing in the late 1800s. They led strikes in mining, railroads and manufacturing for shorter weeks, higher pay, and better working conditions. Twenty-eight different nationalities participated in the 1912 textile mill strike in Lawrence, Massachusetts.

World War I and the Great Depression: Just as the last of the foreign labor was absorbed into the economy, legislation was passed to restrict immigration. In 1917, the first national Immigration Act imposed literacy requirements for entry, created an "Asiatic Barred Zone," and set deportation rules. The purpose of the law was to keep out Eastern and Southern Europeans, who often could not read. The Russian Revolution produced a "Red Scare" in the U.S., resulting in the deportation of 8000 foreign political radicals. In 1921, Congress passed the first Quota Law; with the 1924 National Origins Act, the number of immigrants allowed to come from each country was established, discriminating against people from Southern Europe.

> "Why had the U.S. moved so dramatically to squeeze off the flow of immigrants? First, the U.S. no longer had a labor shortage. The frontier had closed and factories were using complex machinery, cutting the demand for unskilled workers. Second, Americans did not want to compete with foreigners for jobs, especially during the Great Depression of the 1930s."[3]

During the Great Depression, immigration fell to its lowest level in 100 years.

[2] *Ibid*
[3] *Ibid*, p. 7

The Mexicans: The quotas on immigration did not apply to South America. This meant that Mexicans could still enter the U.S. to do work which Americans did not want to do: picking the crops and building the railroads. During the World War II, workers were needed to replace those who had become soldiers. The U.S. government began the *bracero* program which brought Mexican laborers to the U.S. under contract and returned them when they were no longer needed. "The *braceros* were paid 30 cents an hour and often lived in shacks. 'We used to own slaves,' gloated one grower, 'but now we rent them from the government.'" This program continued until 1964.[4]

Recent Policy: In 1952, the Immigration and Nationality Act set national policy on the basis of both economic and political needs. In addition to quotas, special regulations let refugees from communism into the country. The most recent wave of immigration started in the 1960s with a new demand for workers in the South and West. In 1965, the Immigration Act amendments withdrew national quotas and restrictions on Asians, and established preferences for occupations with labor shortages.

Who are the new immigrants? They are mainly Hispanics and Asians, again filling jobs that Americans do not want. For example, between 1970 and 1980, immigrants filled 70% of the new jobs in Los Angeles, but almost all of these were jobs with low wages, little chance for advancement and no job security. Some economists say that there will be an even greater shortage of unskilled workers in the future, and that fewer Americans will be willing to take these jobs. Thus, the same pattern which we have seen so often in American history, may be repeated for immigrants.

Legal Immigrants Admitted to the U.S., by Region of Birth: 1861–1979 (Numbers in percentages of total)

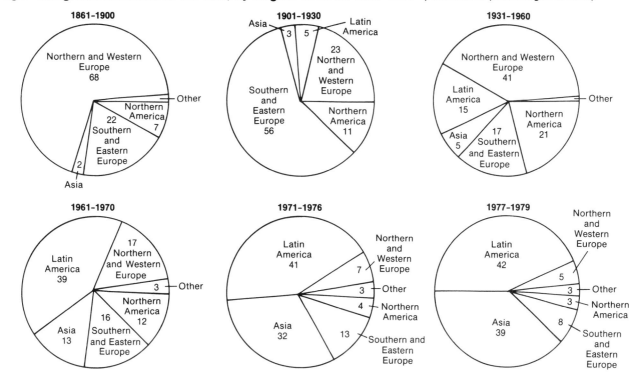

Source: Leon F. Bouvier, *Immigration and Its Impact on U.S. Society*, Population Trends and Public Policy Series No. 2 (Washington, D.C.: Population Reference Bureau, 1981)

[4] *Ibid*, p. 8

Questions for discussion:

1. What kinds of jobs did immigrants fill in different periods of U.S. history?
2. How did Americans react to immigrants in different times?
3. How have immigrants reacted to their role in the U.S. economy?
4. What roles do you see for immigrants in the future?
5. What can immigrants do about their role in the U.S. economy?
6. Add your own questions for discussion.

Lesson 2   The Job Search

CODE

Questions for discussion:

1. What did Manuel think before he came to the U.S.?
What did Manuel do to find a job?
Who is the woman he spoke to? What is her job?
What happened after he filled out the form?
2. Why did the woman say Mr. Smith was busy?
Why did she say Mr. Smith would call?
Do you think Manuel got this job?
3. How do people find jobs in your country?
Have you ever looked for a job in the United States?
What did you do? How long did it take?
Did you get help? Who helped you?
4. Why is it sometimes difficult for immigrants to find jobs?
Are language problems the main reason it is hard?
5. What can you do to find a job?
Who can help you?

THINKING ACTIVITIES

A. OBSTACLES TO FINDING A GOOD JOB

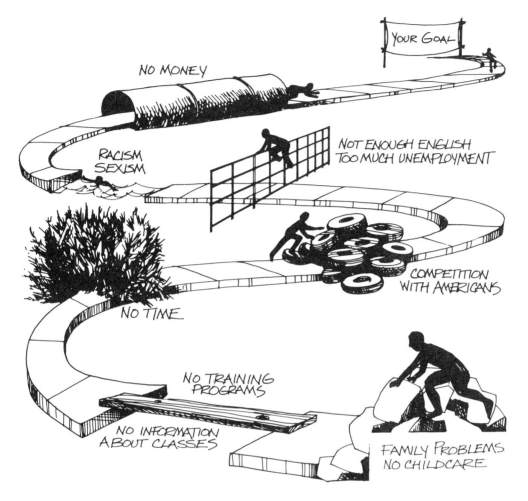

Questions for discussion:

1. What does this person have to do to get to his goal?
What is an obstacle?

2. Are all the problems his fault?
Which are personal problems (his own problems)?
Which are social problems (caused by the society)?

3. What is your goal?
What are some obstacles you have in reaching this goal?
Which obstacles can you do something about?
What obstacles or fears have you had in the past that you don't have now?
   How did you overcome these problems?

4. What obstacles to finding a job do many of you have?
Add to this chart showing personal and social reasons that make it
   hard to find a good job:

Personal	Social
not enough English	not enough jobs
no training	discrimination

5. Which of these problems can you do something about?
What can you do about them?

B. VOCABULARY

Match these words with their meanings.

___ **1.** letter of recommendation	**a.** a time to meet someone	
	b. a form you fill out when you are asking for a job	
___ **2.** job interview		
	c. a paper you give an employer that tells your experience and education	
___ **3.** appointment		
	d. when you and the employer meet to answer questions about the job	
___ **4.** resume		
	e. a letter about you from a former employer	
___ **5.** application		

C. WAYS OF FINDING JOBS

Ask five non-Americans how they got their jobs. Put an X in the right box for each person:

	1	2	3	4	5
Newspaper want ads					
Family or friends					
Employment agencies					
Signs or job postings					
Walk-ins					
Other					

Make a class chart with the results of your interviews.
What are the most common ways people found jobs?

D. INTERVIEWS

Make up *did you* questions for each of these phrases; use them to interview one person about what he or she did to get a job.

1. ask family or friends?
2. go to an employment agency?
3. read signs or job postings?
4. walk into workplaces and ask about jobs?
5. call for an appointment?
6. ask someone to call for you?
7. ask someone to go with you?
8. ask for directions to the place?
9. have an interview?
10. bring a letter of recommendation?
11. bring a resume?
12. fill out an application form?
13. ask questions about the job?
14. call back to check on the job?
15. do anything else?

Grammar Practice (simple past tense): Tell the class what you learned from
your interviews:

> Example: She asked her sister for help.
>   She went to the factory with her sister.

ACTION ACTIVITIES: Competencies

In this book, something you need to know how to do for a job is called
a competency. Here are some job hunting competencies: *asking for help with
directions, filling out forms, reading want ads, answering interview
questions.* The book cannot teach every competency you may need for work.
You and your teacher should work together on competencies that *you* choose.
Which job-finding skills would you like to work on? Choose one competency
to work on with your teacher.

A. COMPETENCY: Finding ads

Most newspapers divide jobs into different categories: general, professional,
sales, medical, business. Bring in your newspaper. Find the categories it uses.

1. List three kinds of job in each category.
2. Where would you look in your paper for these jobs?

factory work	nurse's aide	house painter
teacher's aide	carpenter	hotel housekeeper

3. What job would you like? Where would you find it?

B. COMPETENCY: Reading ads

VOCABULARY
Benefits: Sometimes the employer pays for extra things in addition to your
regular pay: these *benefits* may include sick pay, health insurance, vacation
time, dental insurance.

Requirements or *Qualifications:* The employer may want certain kinds
of experience, education or personal qualities. These *requirements* or
qualifications may include experience, education, and personal traits (like
"energetic person").

Discuss these phrases from ads. Write *R* for requirements and *B* for benefits:

____ must be bilingual   ____ writing skills necessary

____ three years experience   ____ excellent fringe package

____ paid holidays   ____ two weeks vacation

____ must be flexible   ____ masters degree

GETTING INFORMATION FROM ADS: Work with a partner. Cut out two ads from the newspaper and answer these questions:

General information
What kind of work is it?
What is the name of the employer?
Where is the job?

The job
What are the duties? What will you do?
What are the hours? Is it part-time or full-time?
What is the pay?
Are there benefits? What are they?
Is there training?

The applicant (the person who is applying)
What are the requirements?
What kind of person do they want?

How to apply
Do you call, write, or come in person?
Who do you contact?
Where to go or write: What's the address?

Your questions
What do you want to know that is *not* in the ad?

Would you like these jobs? Why or why not? Make a list like this for each job:

Advantages	Disadvantages
good benefits	low pay
I am qualified	too far away

List five reasons you should be hired for this job.

C. COMPETENCY: Finding a job through friends

1. List five friends or relatives who are working in jobs that might be good for you. Ask friends for the names of other people who could help you.
2. What is the name of a place or kind of place you would like to work? Ask friends and relatives to help you find someone who works there:

Place/job	Name	Phone #

3. What do you want to know about this job? List five questions for the person who works there.

> Examples: What is the pay?
> Is there much overtime?

STUDENT ACTION RESEARCH

EVALUATING BOOKS: Look at another ESL book that tells how to find a job. Read the lessons and answer these questions:

1. Does the lesson sound real?
2. What do you like about the lesson? What don't you like?
3. Does the lesson talk about problems finding jobs?
4. Does the lesson teach different ways to find a job?
5. Does the lesson talk about why immigrants sometimes have trouble finding jobs?

LOG: Write a story about looking for work. What happened? How did you start? How did you feel? What problems did you have, if any? How long did you wait? Did you get the job?

Lesson 3   The Job Interview

CODE

Paulo's Interview

Mr. Kim: Have a seat.
Paulo: (*sits down*)
Mr. Kim: I see you were a teacher in Brazil.
Paulo: Yes.
Mr. Kim: Have you ever worked in a factory before?
Paulo: No.
Mr. Kim: Why do you want this job?
Paulo: I need the money.
Mr. Kim: Do you have any experience in electronics?
Paulo: Not yet.
Mr. Kim: Do you have any questions about the job?
Paulo: What is the pay?

Mario's Interview

Mr. Kim: Have a seat.
Mario: Thank you.
Mr. Kim: I see you were a teacher in Brazil.
Mario: Yes, I taught math for ten years.
Mr. Kim: Have you ever worked in a factory?
Mario: No, but I enjoy working with my hands.
Mr. Kim: Why do you want to work here?
Mario: I think I can use my math skills and learn a lot.
Mr. Kim: Do you have any experience in electronics?
Mario: I did a lot of electrical repair work in the army.
Mr. Kim: Do you have any questions about the job?
Mario: Could you tell me a little about the training?

Questions for discussion:

1. What did Paulo do in Brazil?
What did Mario do?
Has Paulo ever worked in a factory? Has Mario?
Do they have the same experience?

2. Are Paulo's answers long or short?
Are Mario's answers long or short?
Do you think Mr. Kim likes Paulo's question? Do you think he likes Mario's question?
Who do you think got the job? Why?

3. Have you ever gone to a job interview? What happened?
Did you ask questions?
Did you get the job?

4. What makes an interview good?
What makes an interview not good?

5. What do you do in a good interview?

THINKING ACTIVITY: Interview chart

What should you do in a job interview? Check the answers you think
are right and then discuss your answers in class.

	always	sometimes	never
1. Smile all the time.	___	___	___
2. Look at the interviewer.	___	___	___
3. Chew gum if you're nervous.	___	___	___
4. Wear a suit and tie (men) or a dress (women).	___	___	___
5. Keep quiet if you don't understand a question.	___	___	___
6. Answer a question even if you don't understand it.	___	___	___
7. Ask a lot about money.	___	___	___
8. Come on time.	___	___	___
9. Refuse to answer a question you don't like.	___	___	___
10. Give short answers.	___	___	___
11. Give long answers.	___	___	___
12. Think about questions before the interview.	___	___	___
13. Ask questions.	___	___	___
14. Dress neatly.	___	___	___
15. Speak softly.	___	___	___
16. (Add your own.)	___	___	___

Make a list of things you should always do; make another list of things
you should never do. Ask your teacher about his or her job interview.
Ask some Americans their opinions about these questions.

ACTION ACTIVITIES

A. COMPETENCY: Answering interview questions

Look at the underlined phrases; most interviews will include these
categories of questions. Discuss questions in each category in pairs.
What does the question mean? What would you answer? What kind of
answer would the interviewer like? Add to the list of questions in each
category.

General opening questions

  Tell me about yourself.
  Why do you want this job?
  Tell me about your background.
  So you're from (*your country*)?

Work experience

What did you do in your country?

I see you were a lawyer in _____.
Have you ever worked in a factory/hotel/school before?
Have you ever done construction/cleaning/electronics work before?
What kinds of work have you done in the U.S.?
Tell me about your experience in construction/nursing . . .
What did you do in your last job?
Tell me about your last job.
Why did you leave your last job?
Why were you unemployed in 1984?

Education

How many years of school have you finished?
How much education have you had?
How long have you studied English?
What kind of training have you had in electronics?

Knowledge of job

Why do you want to work here?
Why are you interested in this job?
What do you know about muffler work?
Why do you think you're qualified for this job?

Work attitudes and personal qualities

Do you work well under supervision?
How do you feel about working overtime?
Do you have transportation? How would you get to work?
What are your strengths? What are your weaknesses?

PRACTICE: Choose an ad for a job you would like. The teacher will interview one person in front of class. Then practice in pairs with questions like the ones listed above.

B. COMPETENCY: Answering difficult questions

GENERAL QUESTIONS: Which questions were hard for you to answer? Why were they difficult? Look at this list of hard questions and add to the list of possible answers for each:

1. Interviewer: I see you haven't worked in two years.
Possible answers: No, I've been in school.
                   I have been working on my English.

Your answer: _____

2. Interviewer: Have you ever done this kind of work?

Possible answer: No, but I have experience in _____
                 (tell about related experience).

3. Interviewer: Why did you drop out of school in the eighth grade?
Possible answer: I had to help my family. I'm working on my GED now.

4. Interviewer: I'm concerned about your English.
Possible answer: I'm taking classes at night now.

5. Add other questions that are difficult for you.
Ask other students for help with possible answers.

WHY DID YOU LEAVE YOUR LAST JOB? What would you answer to this question? Look at the following pairs of reasons for leaving a job. Check the reason that an interviewer would like better. Why?

1. ____ The pay was too low.   ____ I wanted to improve my skills.

2. ____ I wanted to work indoors.   ____ The work was dangerous.

3. ____ I didn't like the hours.   ____ I needed more hours.

4. ____ There were family prob-   ____ I left to take care of my sick
        lems but they are straight-   daughter.
        ened out.

5. ____ I was fired for missing   ____ I had car problems but now
        work.   I have a new car.

6. ____ They wouldn't give me a   ____ I was ready for more
        raise.   responsibility.

7. ____ I got hurt on the job.   ____ I had health problems, but
                                                 I'm fine now.

Have you ever left a job? What was the reason? What would you say about it in an interview?

PERSONAL QUESTIONS: Sometimes interviewers ask personal questions. These questions may be embarrassing or illegal. The law says that employers cannot refuse you a job because of your age, sex, religion, nationality, or country of origin. If they do, it is *discrimination.* Some of these questions may be a sign of possible discrimination. Here are some personal questions; add others to the list.

1. What nationality are you?   **3.** How old are you?
2. What is your religion?   **4.** Are you married?

What would you do if an employer asked you these questions?

1. Answer the question.
2. Answer the question but look for another job.
3. Say nothing.
4. Politely refuse to answer the question.
5. Tell the interviewer that the question is illegal.
6. Other (your idea) _____

What would happen for each of these answers?
What could you say if you did not want to answer a question?

PRACTICE: In pairs, ask each other difficult questions. Try different ways of answering them. Talk about how the interviewer would feel about your answer.

C. COMPETENCY: Asking questions about a job

Interviewers often like it if you ask questions about a job. Why do you think this is true? Your questions usually come near the end of the interview. Start them like this:

		if		
I was wondering	+	when	+	sentence
Could you tell me		how		
		what		

PRACTICE: Change these sentences to a polite form:

1. Is there any overtime?

> Example: I was wondering if there is any overtime.

2. When would I start?   **5.** How often do you give raises?
3. Is there any training?   **6.** Is there a probation period?
4. Are there any benefits?   **7.** Is there medical insurance?

ROLE PLAY: Cut out an ad for a job you might like. Study the information in the ad. Ask another student to interview you for the job with questions from this lesson. Tape the interview. Listen to the tape. Which questions did you answer well? Which questions were hard for you? How could you do better?

EVALUATION

I LIKED:	a lot	so-so	not much
1. Talking about jobs at home/jobs in the U.S.	——	——	——
2. Listing experience, education skills, preferences.	——	——	——
3. Interviewing someone who does a job I might like.	——	——	——
4. Filling out a job application.	——	——	——
5. Researching ways of finding jobs.	——	——	——
6. Finding ads.	——	——	——
7. Reading ads.	——	——	——
8. Evaluating books.	——	——	——
9. Talking about obstacles.	——	——	——
10. Answering interview questions.	——	——	——

I CAN:	easily	sometimes	not at all
1. List my experience.	——	——	——
2. List my education.	——	——	——
3. List my skills.	——	——	——
4. List job preferences.	——	——	——
5. Fill out a job application.	——	——	——
6. Write a resume.	——	——	——
7. Find job ads.	——	——	——
8. Read job ads.	——	——	——
9. Answer interview questions.	——	——	——
10. Ask questions about a job.	——	——	——

I WANT TO: _____

I NEED TO: _____

Starting Work

Lesson 1   The Daily Routine

Naomi Wall

Where does Pei Yi work? She works in a garment factory.
What does she do? She is a stitcher.
What is she doing? She is making linings for jackets.

COLLAGE: Bring in a picture or drawing of yourself at work.

1. Make a collage with pictures of all the students in class.
2. Ask each other about your jobs. Write your occupation under your picture.

Make a chart like this of all the jobs in the class:

PLACE/LOCATION	JOB/OCCUPATION	NAMES
Hospital	housekeeper	Marie, Anna
Hospital	kitchen worker	Mei-zhu
Restaurant	waitress/waiter	Mung Peter

Questions for discussion:

1. What kinds of job do most of the people in the class have?
2. What kinds of job are not on the chart?
3. Does everyone in class work?
4. Is being a student a job? Is being a housewife a job?
5. What do you make or produce?
6. Who do you help in your job?
7. Who needs your work?
8. Why is your job important?

THINKING ACTIVITIES

A. NEW HIRE

Some of the problems new hires have are on the left. Match them with the sentences that have the same meaning.

____ **1.** You run out of supplies.
____ **2.** You can't keep up.
____ **3.** You don't understand directions.
____ **4.** You make a mistake.
____ **5.** You can't remember what to do.
____ **6.** You don't know where something is.
____ **7.** Your supervisor tells you to do your job one way. Your co-workers tell you to do it a different way.
____ **8.** You hurt yourself.
____ **9.** You feel sick.

a. You don't know what to do.
b. You get injured.
c. You are too slow.
d. You don't have enough materials.
e. You do the job wrong.
f. You are told two ways to do the job.
g. You don't feel well.
h. You can't find something you need.
I. You forget what you're supposed to do.

Now answer these questions about each problem:

1. Has this ever happened to you? What did you do?
2. What are three things you could do about this problem?
3. Which is the best of the three choices? Why?
4. What could you say if you had this problem? Whom would you say it to?

B. CHART: I get nervous . . .

Everyone feels uncomfortable sometimes at work. What makes you uncomfortable when you work? What do you do when you're uncomfortable? What *can* you do? Make a chart like this for your class:

What makes you uncomfortable?	What do you do?	What can you do?
Someone talks fast.	Nothing.	Ask them to talk slowly.
I don't know what to do.	Look around.	Ask a co-worker.

Grammar Practice: Make sentences like these about your chart:

> I get nervous when someone talks fast. Usually I do nothing.
> I can ask them to talk slowly.
>
> I get nervous when I don't know what to do. Usually I look around.
> I can ask a co-worker for help.

C. READING: Interviews

Studs Terkel interviewed workers all over America. Here is what some of them said about their work:

> A spot welder said, "I'm a machine."
> "I'm a mule," said a steelworker.
> "A monkey can do what I do," said a receptionist.
> "I'm a robot," said many workers in all different jobs.

Do you ever feel like these workers? Draw a picture of how you feel at work.

Here is what a steel worker named Mike LeFevre said:

The first thing happens at work: When the arms start moving, the brain stops. I punch in about ten minutes to seven in the morning. I say hello to a couple of guys I like, I kid around with them. One guy says good morning to you and you say good morning. . . .

I put on my hard hat, change into my safety shoes, put on my safety glasses, go to the bonderizer. It's the thing I work on. They rake the metal, they wash it, they dip it in a paint solution, and we take it off. Put it on, take it off, put it on, take it off, put it on, take it off. . . .

I say hello to everybody but my boss. At seven it starts. My arms get tired about the first half-hour. After that, they don't get tired any more until maybe the last half-hour at the end of the day. I work from seven to three thirty. My arms are tired at seven thirty and they're tired at three o'clock. I hope to God I never get broke in, because I always want my arms to be tired at seven thirty and three o'clock. (*Laughs.*) Because that's when I know that there's a beginning and there's an end. That I'm not brainwashed. In between I don't even try to think.

—Mike LeFevre, steel worker interviewed by Studs Terkel in *Working*.

D. GETTING THROUGH THE DAY

Make a chart like this that shows some of the things that you like and don't like at work:

Like	Don't like
We can listen to the radio.	We can't hear each other.
We talk while we work.	We can't sit down.
We have fun at lunch.	It's boring.

Finish these sentences to tell what you do when you're bored, tired, angry or happy at work.

When I'm bored, I _____

When I'm angry, I _____

When I'm tired, I _____

When I'm happy, I _____

ACTION ACTIVITY

COMPETENCY: Learning workplace vocabulary

NAMES OF JOBS: How can you find out names of jobs or operations? Add to this list:

> What is this/that job called?
> What are you doing? What is he/she doing?
> What do you call that operation?

NAMES OF TOOLS, PARTS, SUPPLIES OR MATERIALS: How can you find out names of things? Add to this list:

> What is this/that?
> What do you call this/that?
> What's the name of this tool?

PRACTICE: Bring in something from your country that is new to other students. The teacher can also bring in unusual American objects. Other students must find out the object's name by asking questions.

AT WORK: Find out the names of five new things at work (jobs, operations, parts, tools, supplies, etc.). Draw pictures of these things or, *if possible*, take photos of them at work. (Be sure to ask your supervisor for permission to take pictures.) Bring the pictures to class and tell the class the new words.

READING: Long's story

I work at a big hotel in Boston. I am a housekeeper. I go to work at 8:00 on *weekdays* and about 8:30 on weekends. Every week your *schedule* is different. The *manager* decides your days off. Usually everyone wants Saturday and Sunday off.

When I come in, I change into my *uniform* first. Then I *punch in*. After that I get my *bucket* and *room supplies*. They give you a list of rooms to do that day. There are two kinds of rooms: *occupied* and *check-out* rooms. It usually takes

15 or 20 minutes to do an occupied room. It takes more than 30 minutes to do a check-out room. It's a lucky day when all your rooms are occupied. The worst day is when all the rooms are check-out.

In each room, you change the sheets, clean the table, clean the bathroom and put the supplies in order. Usually they give you a five day schedule. But in the winter when it is cold, the *business* of the hotel is slow and they give you a two or three day schedule. We're happy when we have enough hours. We don't like the *slow times.*

ACTIVITIES: Talk about the words in italics and words you don't understand. Circle all the verbs in the simple present tense. Make up questions about the story. Ask each other your questions.

STUDENT ACTION RESEARCH

A. LOG

Write your own story like LeFevre's and Long's. Where do you work? What do you do everyday from the time you come to work to the time you leave? How do you feel about your job?

B. ENGLISH AT WORK

Make a chart of when you use English at work. For one hour, write down every time you listen, speak, read, or write in English. Write down if there is a problem.

Time	Listen	Speak	Read	Write	Problem
8:00	x	x			x
8:15			x		
8:35	x				x
8:50		x			

Discussion: How many times in one hour do you use English at work? Which language skills do you use most? Which skills do you use least? What is hardest for you? What do you need to work on?

C. INTERVIEWS

Use these and other questions to interview someone about his or her job. Copy your questions on a separate sheet of paper, leaving space for the answers. During the interview, write down or tape record the answers:

1. What is your job title?
2. What are your job duties?
3. How long have you been at this job?
4. How did you get this job?
5. What kind of training or experience did you need?
6. What are the most important things you must do to keep this job?
7. What do you like most about working here?

Lesson 2   Talking with Co-workers

CODE

Questions for discussion:

1. What language are the people in box A speaking?
   What language are the people in box B speaking?
   What do the Americans think the Greek workers are saying?

2. How do the Americans feel about the Greeks?
   How do you think the Greeks feel?
   Why do you think they are speaking Greek?

3. Do you ever speak your language at work? When? With whom?
   Do you ever speak English at work? When? With whom?
   Do you have American co-workers?
   How do you feel about talking with American co-workers?
   How do Americans act when you speak your language?
   How do they act when you speak English?

4. Why do Americans sometimes not like it when immigrants speak their
   own language?
   Why do immigrants often like to speak their own language with each other?

5. What do you think the Americans in this picture should do?
   What do you think the immigrants should do?

THINKING ACTIVITY

Discuss each of these situations. Who would you sit with? Who would you ask for help? Why?

1. Two Americans are sitting together at break. They are talking very fast and look upset.
2. An American is sitting by himself reading a book. He always eats by himself and never talks to other workers.
3. Five Americans are sitting together, laughing and talking in loud voices. None of them have ever talked to you before.
4. Two women from your department are sitting together and talking quietly. One of them has helped you with your job before.
5. Describe three people from your job. Which of them could you begin to talk to?

ACTION ACTIVITIES

A. COMPETENCY: Asking for help with a problem

A good way to learn and make friends at the same time is to ask Americans for help with problems. Here are some ways to ask for help. Add to these lists:

Polite opener	Stating the problem	Asking for help
Excuse me.	I'm having trouble with _____	Could you help me?
I'm sorry.	I'm having a hard time with _____	What should I do?
Do you have a minute?	I need some help with _____	Where should I look?
	I can't find _____	
	I'm not sure what to do.	
	I don't know how to _____	
	I ran out of _____	
	There's something wrong with _____	

PRACTICE: Ask for help with these problems:

my tools	finding work gloves
this job	finding safety glasses
the glue	figuring out the directions
this code sheet	fixing my machine
this form	(add your own) _____

B. COMPETENCY: Asking for help with English

You can also explain to someone that you would like help with English; Americans often like to help if they're asked. Add to this list of ways to ask for help with English:

Explanation	Request
I'm trying to learn more English.	Would you mind if I sit with you?
I'm working on my English.	Would it be OK if I ask you for help sometimes?

PRACTICE: Practice asking for help in pairs, using these phrases:

Explanation	Request
1. work on my English	eat lunch with you

> Example: Maria: I'm trying to <u>work on my English</u>. Would
> it be all right if I <u>eat lunch with you</u>
> sometimes?
> Sue: Sure. Anytime. Why don't you sit with us today?

2. improve my English   talk to you
3. practice my English   join you for lunch
4. learn more English   ask you questions

C. COMPETENCY: Handling problems with co-workers

Read these problems and rank the solutions from best (1) to worst. In small groups, discuss your answers and choose a group solution. Explain your group solution to the class.

1. Two workers need scissors; they are on piece work and can't make money without scissors. The foreman brings one pair of scissors.

_____ They should share the scissors.

_____ They should complain and ask for another pair.

_____ One worker should take the scissors quickly.

_____ (other) _____

2. A worker sees that his co-workers never wear safety glasses. They know the rules. He thinks they might get hurt.

_____ He should tell the foreman.

_____ He shouldn't say anything.

_____ He should tell them to put on their glasses.

_____ He should ask them why they never wear glasses.

_____ (other) _____

3. Add your own problem with co-workers and discuss it. What are your choices? What is the best choice? Why?

READING: Hien's story

When I put my first step on the soil of this country, like thousands of Indochinese refugees who came here, I believed my life would be better. I thought the peace, freedom of this country would help me to forget all the bad memories of experiences in my country. The first time when I came to work, I strongly believed that, but right now I know a lot of problems exist for the people who work with no English.

From my earliest experiences at work I learned that I was nobody without English. I stood in line at a sandwich shop more than one month making the same order every day at lunch: hamburger. That was the only word I could speak correctly. I wanted to order something else but a lot of people were in line and if the cook couldn't understand what I said, he would ask me again and the people in line would get angry with me.

At work, I kept silence. When my fellow workers talked, I didn't share my feelings with them, not even a smile. At break time, I chose a separate place for myself. When my manager asked me, "Why don't you talk with people?" he got my answer, "How can I?" In the eyes of my fellow workers, I became a strange person.

But I was luckier than other workers who can't speak English. At least my fellow workers respected my silence. My friend told me a story about his job. He worked for a house repair team. This team had two groups of workers, wood workers and helpers. The rule in the helper group was that if someone came first, they got the work first and later people did another job. When the winter came, nobody wanted to work outside. My friend came early, but another who was late took his tools and told him to go to work outside. My friend was angry because his fellow worker didn't have the right to do that. That was unfair but he couldn't complain to his boss because he couldn't speak English. The same thing happened a few times and he fought with his fellow worker and he got fired. I know a lot of fighting between Indochinese workers and their fellow workers happens because of the barrier of English.

When you work and don't understand English, you don't know the value of your work and your rights. Another friend works in a seafood company. He began with the starting salary. After six months, he asked for a raise and his boss answered him, "We can't give you a raise because you can't speak English." What was wrong with him because he couldn't speak English? Could he not finish his job well? I know he is a good worker who works a lot of overtime.

The first time when I came to work, I brought the hope of a better life in my work. But right now, I know where is the place that this country gives for people who work with no English. I really don't like this position but I have no choice.

Questions for discussion:

1. What happened to Hien because he couldn't speak English?
   What happened to his friends?
2. How does Hien feel?
   What does he say is the place for people with no English in this country?
   Do you agree or disagree with him?
3. Think of one time when you needed to say something in English but
   could not. What did you want to say?
   What did you do? What happened then?

LOG: Add to Hien's story or tell your story to the teacher. He or she will add some of the stories to the Log.

STUDENT ACTION RESEARCH: Talking with co-workers

OBSERVE: Which workers do you talk to at work every day? What do you talk to them about? What language do you use?

RECORD: Make a chart like the one below which lists each worker you talk to on *one day*. Write their names, what language you spoke and what you talked about. You may want to take a notebook to work with you and take notes while you're working.

Name	Language	Topic
Maria	Spanish	Kids, work
John	English	Supplies, weather
Jim	English	Weekend, movies

ANALYZE: Do you notice any patterns? Do you only speak English when you talk about work? Do you only talk to non-American workers about your family? Who do you *not* talk to? What would you like to work on with your teacher? Make a list like this one:

> Talk to Americans about schools.
> Talk to Americans about family.
> Talk to Americans about sports.
> Talk to Americans about job problems.

Lesson 3 Talking with the Boss

CODE

Questions for discussion:

1. What is the boss telling Rajan?
Do you think Rajan understands him?

2. What is the problem here?
Why does Rajan say yes?
What do you think will happen next?

3. Do you ever have trouble with directions?
What do you do?
What other language problems do you have with the boss?
Have you ever needed help but *not* asked for it?
   Why didn't you ask?

4. Why is it difficult for Rajan to understand?
What kinds of language problems do foreign workers have with their
   bosses?

5. What should Rajan do?
What can you do if there is a language problem?

THINKING ACTIVITY: Identifying communication problems

Some supervisors were interviewed about the immigrants and refugees at their workplaces. Here are some of their comments. Do you think your boss might say this about you?

Supervisors' comments	YES	NO
1. "They don't tell me when they can't understand."	___	___
2. "They don't ask questions about directions."	___	___
3. "They don't tell me about problems."	___	___
4. "They don't know the names of tools and parts."	___	___

Supervisors' comments	YES	NO
5. "They get very upset when I say they made a mistake."	___	___
6. "They don't talk to other workers."	___	___
7. "They smile when I am angry."	___	___

ACTION ACTIVITIES: Directions

A. COMPETENCY: Understanding directions

Look at these different ways of giving the same directions.

> Lock each room when you're done!
> *Be sure to* lock each room when you're done.
> *You have to* lock each room when you're done.
> *You should* lock each room when you're done.
> *You* lock each room when you're done.

PRACTICE: Give directions using these phrases:

1. turn this knob
2. connect these wires
3. put the supplies in here
4. read the code
5. return the tools to me
6. report to the team leader
7. replace broken pieces
8. let me know about problems

B. COMPETENCY: Asking for help with directions

What can you say if you don't understand directions? Add to this list:

What can you say if you don't understand one part of a sentence? Ask about the italicized words in sentences 1 to 7.

1. Tell your foreman I need to *borrow* you.

> Examples: You need to *what*?
>   Tell him *what*?
>   What does *borrow* mean?

2. On the seventh line, fill in your *country of origin*.
3. After you finish set up, check the *code sheet*.
4. If the cord is *frayed*, don't use it.
5. Check to be sure all the *fire extinguishers* are in place.
6. I'm going to put you on *light duty*.
7. You can sign up for Blue Cross or the *HMO*.

C. COMPETENCY: Giving feedback about directions

UNDERSTANDING THE PROBLEM: Divide into nationality groups in your class. Act out this story. What do you think Hung does at the end? What would you do in your country? Add your own endings and explain them:

Mr. Smith: Before you start today, please check your supplies. You may not have enough wax.

Hung: (*smiles*)

Mr. Smith: (*loud voice*) I said, check your supplies before you start. You may need wax.

Hung: (*silence*)

Mr. Smith: (*yelling*) DO YOU HAVE ENOUGH WAX?

Hung: Yes, I already checked.

Questions for discussion:

1. Why does Mr. Smith use a loud voice and yell?
2. Why is Hung quiet at first?
3. How does Mr. Smith feel?
4. How does Hung feel?
5. What is the problem here?
6. In your country, do you always respond to directions?
7. What do you do in your country when a supervisor is angry?
8. What were the differences between your endings?
9. How could Hung prevent this problem? What should he do?

GIVING FEEDBACK: Often people want to know if you understand them. Here are some ways to show them. Add to these lists of questions and short answers:

Question	Feedback		
Do you understand?	Yes, I do.	or	No, I *don't*.
Did you get that?	_____	or	_____
Are you following?	_____	or	_____
Was that clear?	_____	or	_____

Directions	Feedback
Be sure to shut each door.	OK, I will.
Report to the loading dock.	All right.

Practice: Respond to these directions:

1. Check your supplies before you start today.
2. Be sure to punch out when you leave work.
3. Your relief man will tell you when you get a break.
4. Before you leave, check in with me.
5. Go to Personnel; they need your signature.

THINKING ACTIVITIES: Reporting problems

A. UNDERSTANDING PROBLEMS

Act out this story and add your own ending:

Mr. Smith: What happened to the windows in back? Only half of them are clean.

Rajan: I couldn't reach the top.

Mr. Smith: Why didn't you ask for a ladder?

Rajan: I'm sorry. I thought you would be angry.

Mr. Smith: Well, I am angry now. You should have asked.

Questions for discussion:

1. Why were some windows dirty? Why didn't Rajan clean them?
2. Why didn't he ask for a ladder? How did he feel?
3. How does Mr. Smith feel? What is he angry about?
4. Did you ever have a problem like this at work?
5. What did you do?
6. Did you ever get in trouble for reporting a problem? What happened?

B. REPORTING PROBLEMS

Here are some problems. Do you think you should tell your supervisor about them?

	yes	no	maybe/ sometimes		yes	no	maybe/ sometimes
1. You run out of supplies.	___	___	___	**7.** You think your boss is treating you unfairly.	___	___	___
2. You need to go to the doctor during work.	___	___	___	**8.** You broke your machine.	___	___	___
3. You feel sick.	___	___	___	**9.** You think your paycheck is wrong.	___	___	___
4. You can't keep up with the work.	___	___	___	**10.** You see another worker leaving early.	___	___	___
5. You don't understand part of the job.	___	___	___	**11.** You make a mistake.	___	___	___
6. You see another worker stealing.	___	___	___	**12.** (Add your own.)	_____		

Questions for discussion:

1. What will happen if you report each of these problems?
2. Will your supervisor be angry? Will other workers be angry?
3. Will you get in trouble? Will your supervisor be glad? Will your supervisor help you?
4. If you don't tell your boss, who should you tell: nobody, another worker, a union representative, or someone else?

C. ORGANIZATION CHARTS

Make a chart like this one of people that you work with. What do they do?
Who is their boss? Who do they report problems to?

Person	Job	Boss
Me, Maria	assemblers	Anna
Sofia	inspector	Anna
Anna	forelady	Mr. Smith
Mr. Smith	supervisor	Mr. Jones
Mr. Jones	manager	?????

Draw a diagram of the reporting system of your workplace. Who is at the top?
Who do you think owns your workplace? Who has the most responsibility?
Who decides what happens?

ACTION ACTIVITY

COMPETENCY: Reporting a problem

To report a problem, use a *polite opener, state the problem,* and *ask for help.*
Add to these lists:

Polite opener	Stating the problem	Asking for help
Excuse me.	My machine is broken.	What should I do?
I have a problem.	I need the ladder.	Do you know where it is?

Practice: Report each of these problems to someone. Tell whom you would
ask for help.

1. Your machine isn't working.

> Example: Worker: Excuse me. Do you have a minute?
> Supervisor: What's up?
> Worker: My machine isn't working. Could you help
> me with it?

2. You ran out of screws and don't know where to get them.

3. Your screwdriver is broken and you can't do your job.

4. You feel sick to your stomach.

5. You can't remember what to do.

6. You couldn't wax the floors because you ran out of wax.

7. You don't know how to turn off your machine.

8. (Add some real problems from your job.) _____

STUDENT ACTION RESEARCH

OBSERVE: What do you talk to your supervisor about? What do you ask or tell your supervisor? What does your supervisor ask or tell you?

RECORD: Take notes about what you talk to your boss about in one day.

I ask/tell him/her about	He/she asks/tells me about
not enough parts	storeroom
bathroom break	mistake in my work

REPORT: What did you talk about? Were there any problems? What do you need or want to talk to your supervisor about?

LOG: Write about any problems talking with your supervisor. What happened? Did you get upset? Did your supervisor get upset? Do you know why? Discuss the problem in class; put some of the stories into the log.

EVALUATION

Look back at this unit. Discuss what you liked, what you didn't like, what you learned and what you want to learn. Use the same chart for future units.

I LIKED:	a lot	so-so	not much
1. _____	___	___	___
2. _____	___	___	___
3. _____	___	___	___
4. _____	___	___	___
5. _____	___	___	___
6. _____	___	___	___
7. _____	___	___	___

I CAN:	easily	sometimes	not at all
1. _____	___	___	___
2. _____	___	___	___
3. _____	___	___	___
4. _____	___	___	___
5. _____	___	___	___
6. _____	___	___	___
7. _____	___	___	___

I WANT TO:

1. _____

2. _____

I NEED TO:

1. _____

2. _____

Making Money

Lesson 1   Pay

CODE

Chiang: What's the matter?

Lee: My check is too small. It's about $10 short.

Chiang: Maybe they took out union dues.

Lee: I don't think so. It's not on the check stub.

Chiang: Did you miss any time?

Lee: I was five minutes late, but they took out more than that.

Chiang: Why don't you ask your supervisor?

Lee: Do you think I should? Maybe it's my mistake.

Questions for discussion:

1. What is Lee's problem? Why is he worried?
What does Chiang think might have happened?
What is a *check stub*?
Did Lee miss any work?

2. What does Chiang tell Lee to do?
How does Lee feel about talking to his supervisor?

3. How do you get paid? By the hour, piecework, or salary?
Has your pay ever been wrong? Why? What did you do?
Did you ever lose pay because you were late? How much?
Do you think $10 is a big mistake or a little mistake?

4. What are some reasons for small checks?
What are some reasons that checks might be wrong?
What do you think is a good wage?
What do you think is enough to live on?

5. What do you think Lee should do?
Do you think you should always ask about mistakes in checks? When do
   you think you should ask?
Who can you ask about problems with paychecks?
What can you do if your wage is not good?

THINKING ACTIVITIES

A. THE WAGE SYSTEM

VOCABULARY: Match these different ways of getting paid with their
meanings:

1. hourly rate ＿＿ The employer pays a yearly rate, which is divided into
                      weekly, bi-weekly or monthly checks.
2. piece rate   ＿＿ The employer sets a base rate of pay for each hour
                      of work and multiplies it by the number of hours
                      worked each week.
3. salary   ＿＿ The employer sets a rate for each piece of work and
                      multiplies by the number of pieces.

COMPARING PAY SYSTEMS: What do you like about your pay system?
What don't you like? Make a chart like this:

	Good	Bad
Piece Rate:	can make more money	hurry, hurry, hurry broken machine—no money
Hourly Rate:	same pay every week	can't make more

Discuss these questions for each system:

1. Who sets the base rate (for piecework) or the wage (for hourly)?
2. Who changes the rate/wage? Why?
3. How can you make more money?
4. What happens if you can't work fast?
5. What happens if your machine breaks or you need a tool?
6. What problems do you have with other workers?

B. PAY STUBS

What are some reasons to save pay stubs? Add to this list:

> To get food stamps
> To get financial aid
> To figure out pay problems

				PRVA 3694856380 02-19-85 CHECK NO. 188497		
LUI. MEIZHU			8311	BASE RATE OF SALARY ► 6.3038	AMT. OF CHECK ►	19800
EARNINGS	TAXES	DEDUCTIONS	NET PAY	DESCRIPTION	TAXES/DED.	YEAR-TO-DATE
26015 –	3953 –	2262 =	19800	FEDERAL TAX	2865	24546
227468 –	34056 –	19768 =	173644	STATE TAXES	1088	9510
DESCRIPTION	HOURS	EARNINGS	YEAR-TO-DATE	RETIRE 7%	1821	15922
REGULAR	4000	25215	208339	COUNCIL 93	300	2700
WKEND/H OLIDAY		800	4000	CHARITY	100	900
				HCHP FAM	41	246

STATEMENT OF EARNINGS AND DEDUCTIONS • DETACH AND RETAIN FOR YOUR RECORDS

ACTION ACTIVITIES

A. COMPETENCY: Reading pay stubs

VOCABULARY: Discuss each word and find the item on Mei-zhu's pay stub. Then answer the questions for your own or a friend's pay stub.

pay period: the dates that the check covers.

> What is the pay period of Mei-zhu's check?

hours: the number of hours you worked in this pay period.

> How many hours did she work?
> How many hours did she get paid for?

type/description of pay: the kind of time your check covers—regular time, overtime, vacation, sick time, holidays, personal days.

> What kinds of pay did she get?
> How many hours were sick pay?

base rate: the regular amount you get paid for each hour of work, each piece, or each pay period.

> What is her base rate of pay?

gross pay: your total pay or earnings for all the work you do plus overtime, holiday, vacation, sick pay.

What is her gross pay?

deductions: money taken out of your gross pay. Some deductions come out of every check (like taxes); others are *optional* (you can choose to have money taken out for things like the credit union or charity). Discuss each deduction: What is it for? How does it help you?

state and federal taxes　　credit union
social security (FICA)　　charity (like United Way)
pension contributions　　health insurance
union dues　　health and welfare fund

What deductions were taken out of Mei-zhu's check?
How much was deducted for taxes?
How much was deducted for other contributions?

net pay: your take-home pay after deductions are taken out of your gross pay; the amount on your check.

What is her net pay?

B. COMPETENCY: Calculating pay

In small groups, figure out the following worker's pay for the week. Compare your answers.

Hourly rate: $5.50
Number of hours worked: 　32 regular
　　　　　　　　　　　　8 sick pay
　　　　　　　　　　　　4 overtime (1 1/2 times regular pay)

Gross pay: _____

Deductions:		
	Federal taxes	19.83
	State taxes	7.70
	FICA	10.15
	Blue Cross/Blue Shield	25.40
	Union dues	5.50
	Total	_____

Net pay: _____

PRACTICE: Now make up problems for each other using information from your own checks.

" It broke down figuring out one of
our piece-workers' wages..."

THINKING ACTIVITY: Pay problems

Raoul: Where's my check?
Supervisor: We always pay cash.
Raoul: But this is only $121. I should get $150 for five days.
Supervisor: Yes, but I had to take taxes out.

Questions for discussion:

1. How does Raoul get paid?
2. What does working "under the table" mean?
3. What is Raoul's problem?
4. What is the supervisor's reason for paying $121?
5. What do you think happened to Raoul's money?
6. Why do some employers like to pay cash?
7. Why do some workers like to be paid in cash?
8. What problems may happen if you are paid in cash?
9. What do you think Raoul should do?

READING: Wage laws

Divide into groups and read about wage laws. Each group should read one of the numbered sections and report to the others.

1. *The law says:* You must be paid the wages and salaries you have earned.

   This means: Your employer cannot keep your pay if he is short of money.
   Your employer cannot take away an hour's pay if you were five minutes late.
   Your employer must pay you for all wages, vacation pay, and holiday pay that you earned if you leave a job.

2. Each state has its own wage laws. Most states have laws that workers must be paid *promptly*, *regularly*, and *in full*.

   This means: Your employer must pay you on time, not late.
   Your employer must pay every week if you are an hourly worker or a piece worker.
   Your employer cannot keep money he owes you.

3. *Docking:* When an employer takes money out of your check, it's called *docking* you. It is legal for employers to dock you for some things but it is illegal to dock you for others.

   For example, in Massachusetts, an employer *can* dock you if:

   —you charge a customer the wrong amount.
   —you add up a bill incorrectly.
   —you are the only one working at a cash register and money is missing at the end of your shift.

   In Massachusetts, the employer *cannot* reduce your check if:

   —many people use one cash register and money is missing.
   —a customer leaves without paying.
   —a machine breaks so you cannot work (except if the employer sends you home).

—there are not enough parts and you have to wait for them.

—the employer accuses you of "poor work" or "mistakes" or "damage to property."

4. In Massachusetts, an employer who violates the weekly wage law can be fined up to $500 or go to jail for up to two months.

ACTION ACTIVITIES: Pay problems

COMPETENCY: Reporting a pay problem

Many pay problems can be corrected by talking to your employer. Start with a *polite opener*, *state the problem* or *ask a question*, then *respond to the answer*. Add to these lists:

Polite opener

Excuse me.	I have a question about my check.
Do you have a minute?	I'd like to talk to you about my check.

State the problem/ask a question

I worked two hours overtime, but it's not on the check.
Why did I get docked twenty minutes?

Respond to the answer

You may get a *positive* answer:

Supervisor:	Worker:
I'll look into it.	Thank you very much.
I'll correct that.	When will I find out?
I'll check it out.	When will it be in my check?

Or you may get a *negative* answer:

You were docked for being late.
You don't get any more sick time.
You don't get paid when the machine is down.

What could you do if the response is negative? Add to this list and discuss each answer.

____ Argue with your boss.

____ Check your adding and your records.

____ Ask another worker for help.

____ Get a lawyer.

____ Forget it.

ROLE PLAY: Act out what you would do for each of these pay problems: Who would you talk to? What would you say? What response might you get? What would you say if you got a positive answer (i.e., I'll look into it)? What would you say if you got a negative answer (i.e., You don't get any more sick time)?

1. Your check is small but you don't know why.
2. You put in for a sick day but it's not on your check.
3. Your boss docked you because some cash was missing.
4. You didn't get paid while your machine was broken.
5. Your boss is having a problem and says he'll pay you next week.

STUDENT ACTION RESEARCH

Find out about the wage laws in your state. Whom can you ask about them? Invite someone to class to talk about them. Add to these questions:

1. Can the employer dock you if a customer leaves without paying?
2. Can the employer dock you for poor work?
3. What will happen to an employer who violates the wage law?
4. What can you do if your employer violates the wage laws?

THE MINIMUM WAGE LAWS: Current federal law says that most workers must be paid at least $3.35 an hour. Find out more about the minimum wage laws:

1. Who is covered?
2. What is the minimum wage for agricultural workers?
3. What is the minimum wage for workers who get tips?
4. Who can be paid less than the minimum wage?
5. Who enforces the minimum wage laws?
6. What happens to an employer who violates them?

A GUIDE TO PROBLEM-POSING

In every lesson, we follow the same process: naming a problem, discussing it, finding out more about it, working with others to understand it and think of ways to change it, thinking about the results of the actions and taking action to make small changes. Follow these steps to look at one problem in your workplace or class.

CODE-WRITING

Each lesson starts with a conversation or code about a common problem of immigrant workers. Then there are discussion questions in five steps:

1. What is happening in the conversation or code?
2. What is the problem? How do the people in the code feel?
3. Have you had a problem like this? What happens in your country about this situation?
4. Why did this happen? What are the reasons for this kind of problem? What are its social and economic causes? Why do many people have this problem?
5. What can be done about the problem? What are the choices?

FINDING RESOURCES AND TAKING ACTION

These questions can help you with the process of taking action to address the problem:

1. What do you need to know to change the problem?
2. Who can you work with to find out new information? Where can you get more information?
   —What do your co-workers say about the problem?
   —What does your boss say?
   —What does the law say about the problem?
   —What does your union say?
   —What do other organizations or outsiders say?
3. What can you do about the problem? How can you work with others to change the situation? What can you do legally?
4. What might happen if you try?

EVALUATING YOUR ACTIONS

After you take action about a problem, you can ask these questions:

1. What new information did we learn about the issue? What do we understand better now?
2. What did I learn about myself?
3. What did we learn about how we work as a group?
4. What was the result or impact of our action? How was it successful? What could we do differently next time?
5. Can we address the causes of the problem better now?
6. What new problems or issues did we uncover?

Lesson 2   Benefits

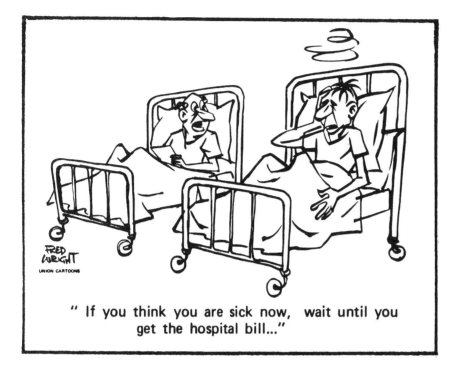

" If you think you are sick now, wait until you
get the hospital bill..."

CODE

Alex: This is my last day here.

George: How come? Where are you going?

Alex: I got a job in a restaurant. It pays more.

George: Will you get the same benefits?

Alex: No, but I need the money.

George: What about insurance?

Alex: I'm never sick. And I'll get $1.00 an hour more.

George: Money isn't everything.

Alex: But I need the money to feed my family.

Questions for discussion:

1. What is Alex going to do?
   Why does he want to change jobs?
   What does George ask him?
   Will Alex get insurance in his new job?
2. What are benefits?
   Why does George think they are important?
   Why does Alex think money is more important?

3. In your country, do workers get benefits? What are they?
In your country, what happens if a worker gets sick?
Who pays for the hospital? Does the worker get sick leave?
Have you ever been in the hospital in the U.S.?
Who paid for the hospital? Did you get paid for sick days?
Do you have benefits at your job? Do you know your benefits?

4. What do you think is more important—money in your check or benefits?
What can happen if you have no benefits?
What can happen if you don't have enough money?

5. Do you think it is good to change jobs for a little more money?
What do you think Alex should do?

THINKING ACTIVITIES

A. IDENTIFYING BENEFITS

Benefits are extra things that your employer pays for in addition to wages.
Benefits in each workplace are different. Some jobs have no benefits.
In small groups, discuss each benefit and match it with its definition.
Do workers in your country get this benefit?

1. paid vacations   _____ The employer pays if you are not able to work because of illness or accident.

2. paid holidays   _____ The company pays part or all of your medical insurance.

3. personal days   _____ The company pays for a certain number of days off that you do not have to explain.

4. sick or disability pay   _____ The company pays for a week or more vacation.

5. health insurance   _____ The company pays for insurance to cover work on your teeth.

6. dental insurance   _____ The company pays for time off on holidays.

7. pension/retirement plan   _____ The company gives you time off when you have a baby.

8. training   _____ The company puts some money into a special account that you will get when you retire/stop working.

9. life insurance   _____ The company pays for insurance that your family will get if you die.

10. maternity leave*   _____ The company will give you special training to improve your skills (like free English classes or training for a better job).

11. education   _____ The company will pay for your classes away from the workplace to improve your job skills.

*Unit VI, Lesson 5 talks more about maternity benefits.

B. INTERVIEWS

Interview your teacher or a friend about the benefits he or she receives.
If you are working, find out the answers for your own job. Add to this list
of questions about each benefit.

Vacation
Do you get paid vacation time? If so, how much?
Do you choose your vacation time or does the employer tell you when
    to go on vacation?
Do you get paid for vacation if you don't take it?

Holidays
Do you get paid holidays? If so, which holidays?
Do you get extra pay if you work on holidays? How much?

Personal Days
Do you get paid personal days? If so, how many?
Do you need to tell your employer *before* you take a personal day?

Sick Days/Disability Pay
Do you get paid sick days? If so, how many?
Do you get paid for them if you don't take them?
Do you get disability pay if you are sick for a long time?

Health Insurance
Does your employer pay for health insurance?
How much does the employer pay? How much do you pay?
Can you choose your health plan?

Pension
Does your employer have a pension fund?
How much does the employer pay? How much do you pay?

Education and Training
Does your employer pay for training outside the workplace?
What kind of courses are paid for?
How do you get this benefit?
Does your employer have any special training programs in the workplace?
    How can you get into them?

Other benefits
Do you have any other benefits? If so, what are they?

C. ADVANTAGES AND DISADVANTAGES

It is not always enough to think just about the pay or benefits in a job.
Sometimes there are hidden *advantages* and *disadvantages*. Match each
word or phrase with its meaning.

1. shift   _____ extra hours of work

2. shift differential   _____ more money for the same work

3. overtime   _____ extra pay to keep up with inflation
                                                (higher costs)

4. raise   _____ regular time of work

5. promotion   _____ move to a better job

6. cost of living increase/   _____ extra money for later shift
       adjustment

Add to these lists of questions about advantages and disadvantages:

Location
Is the job close to home?
How much does it cost you to get to work?

Hours
Are the hours good for you and your family?
Is there a shift differential?
Is there overtime? Do you have to work overtime?

Raises
How often do you get raises?
How much are the raises?
Do you get a cost of living raise?

Promotions
Is there a chance of promotion?
How do you get a promotion?

D. CHOOSING JOBS

Everyone has different needs: for some people, money in the pocket is important; for others, insurance is more important. In small groups, look at each worker's story and choose the best job for him or her. Discuss your answers.

JOB #1: Factory work: second shift, much overtime, good pay but very few benefits.

JOB #2: Office cleaning work: third shift (11:00 p.m. to 7:00 a.m.), low pay, good insurance, paid holidays and vacation, no overtime.

JOB #3: Hotel work: first shift, average pay, good benefits including life insurance, health insurance, and dental, but little chance for promotion.

JOB #4: Hospital work: changing schedule, some weekend and holiday work, average pay, poor benefits, no overtime.

1. Jose has no family in the U.S. He lives with some friends and wants to earn money quickly to send to his family in Guatemala.

He should choose JOB #____.

2. Maria is a single parent with three children in the U.S. She lives with a friend who helps with the rent. Her children go to school at 8:00 and come home at 3:30.

She should choose JOB #____.

3. Hien is in college. He needs to work to pay for school. He lives with three friends and gets insurance at his college. He needs time to study.

He should choose JOB #____.

4. Mr. Gonzales is in his late fifties. He has three children. His wife works part-time with no benefits. He has a part-time job at night.

He should choose JOB #____.

5. You: Which job would be best for you? Why?
Which benefits are most important for you?

ACTION ACTIVITY

COMPETENCY: Asking for a raise

Before asking for a raise, you should find out the procedures for raises at your workplace:

1. Are raises automatic after a certain amount of time?
2. How often do employees get raises?
3. Are raises in the contract (if you have a union)?
4. Can you get extra raises for good work?
5. Who can give you a raise?

Act out the following dialogue and identify when the worker *makes the request*, *states length of employment*, and *explains the reason* for wanting a raise.

Worker: Do you have time to talk?

Supervisor: What's the problem?

Worker: I'd like to talk about getting a raise.

Supervisor: How long have you been here?

Worker: For a year and a half.

Supervisor: Didn't you get a raise six months ago?

Worker: Yes, I did.

Supervisor: We only give raises once a year.

Worker: But you've given me more work and responsibility. I've been training the other workers.

Supervisor: Well, I'll check with the manager.

Worker: Thanks. I'll check back with you in a few days.

Add to this list of ways to ask for a raise:

Making the request
I was wondering when I'll get a raise.
Could we talk about my pay?

Stating length of employment

I've been here _____ months.

Explaining the reason for the request
I have more responsibility now. I train other workers.

I do the same thing that _____ does and he makes _____.

ROLE PLAY: Act out asking for a raise in these situations.

1. You've worked at your place a year without a raise.
2. You have extra medical expenses and will have to get another job if you don't get a raise.
3. Do you think you deserve a raise? Act out your request.

STUDENT ACTION RESEARCH

If you are working, find some benefits you want to know more about; make a list of questions to ask at work. Who can you ask at work? Find the answers and report back. *If you are not working*, think about what is important for you in a job. (Do you want sick days? health insurance?) Make a list of questions you could ask in a job interview.

Lesson 3   Overtime

UE News

CODE

Donaldo: They want us to work late today.

Mark: Again? I'm tired of this overtime. Forty hours a week is enough.

Donaldo: Don't you like the money?

Mark: Of course, I do. But I have things to do. I never see my kids. I need to do some work around the house. And I need my *sleep*.

Donaldo: You'll never get ahead that way. The best thing you can do for your kids is bring home a big check.

Questions for discussion:

1. What do these workers have to do today?
   What does Mark want to do?
   What does Donaldo want to do?
2. Why does Mark want to go home?
   Why does Donaldo want to stay?
   How does Donaldo think Mark can help his children?
3. In your country, how long was the work day?
   Did you ever work overtime? Did you get extra pay?
   Do you ever work overtime in the U.S.?
   Do you have to work overtime? Can you choose?
4. Do you like overtime? Why or why not? What are the advantages and
   disadvantages of overtime?
   How does working overtime help your family? How does spending time
   with them help your family? Which do you think is more important?
   Why do people have to choose between working overtime and spending
   time with their families?
5. What can you do if you don't want to work overtime?
   What can you do if you want more overtime?
   What are some overtime problems? What can you do about them?

READING: Overtime Regulations

Answer true or false to the following statements.

1. In every job, the employer must pay you overtime
   if you work more than 40 hours a week.   _____
2. In every job, the employer must give everyone the
   same number of hours of overtime.   _____
3. In every job, you must work overtime if your boss
   asks you to.   _____
4. All the rules for overtime are the same for every job.   _____
5. The laws about overtime are the same all over the
   United States.   _____

Now read about overtime laws to check your answers. Divide into groups;
each group should read one question and report on it to the class.

1. Who decides overtime regulations? Some rules for overtime are the same
everywhere: rules about pay for overtime are set by the federal government.
Other rules are different: the amount of overtime is different in each job. In
some jobs you must work overtime if the supervisor asks you. This is called
mandatory overtime. In other jobs you can refuse overtime. This is called
optional overtime. In some jobs the employer must offer the same amount of
overtime to all workers. In other jobs this is not true.

2. Who do federal laws cover? These laws cover almost all hourly and piece-
rate workers and many who get salaries. They do *not* cover everyone. Here are
some of the workers they do not cover:

Supervisors   Employees of railroads and air carriers
Workers in seasonal businesses   Employees of small hotels and restaurants
Fishers and farmworkers   (with less than $362,500 revenue per year)

3. What do the overtime laws say? Employers must pay workers one and one-half times their regular rate of pay for all hours worked over 40 hours each week. This means if you work 48 hours in one week, your employer must pay you time and a half for 8 hours. Employers may not average weeks together. This means if you work 48 hours this week and 32 hours next week, you must still be paid 8 hours of overtime.

4. What do the federal overtime laws NOT say?

The law does not say: There is a limit on the daily or weekly hours of work. *This means:* The law does not say how many hours you can work each day or week.*

The law does not say: Employers must pay for hours worked over eight in a day.

This means: If you work 10 hours one day but only 6 hours another day, and your weekly total is still 40 hours, your employer does not have to pay overtime.

The law does not say: Your employer must pay extra for weekend or holiday work.*

This means: If you work on a holiday instead of another day, your employer doesn't have to pay overtime.

The law does not say: Your employer has to pay for rest periods, holidays, or vacations.*

THINKING ACTIVITIES

A. CHECK YOURSELF

What do the federal overtime laws say? Write true or false for each of these statements.

1. Employers must pay overtime for holidays. _____
2. Employers must pay overtime for more than 8 hours of work in one day. _____
3. Employers usually must pay overtime for more than 40 hours of work in one week. _____
4. Employers may average the number of hours you worked in two weeks to figure your pay. _____
5. Most hourly workers are covered by the overtime laws. _____
6. Overtime pay is one and a half times regular pay. _____

B. OVERTIME PROBLEMS

CHUNG CHI'S PROBLEM: Chung Chi is a bus driver for the city. His supervisor asked him to work twelve hours each day for several weeks. The city needed extra drivers while the subway was being fixed. Chung Chi said yes because his boss needed help. He did not want trouble with his boss. After two weeks, Chung Chi's union representative told him to stop working overtime. The union contract says no more than two hours overtime each day. Chung Chi stopped working overtime. He did not want trouble with the union.

*Your employer may have to pay overtime because of state laws or contract regulations, even though federal laws don't cover these areas.

Questions for discussion:

1. Why did Chung Chi's boss want him to work overtime?
2. How many hours did he work each day?
3. Why did he work overtime?
4. What did the union representative say to Chung Chi?
5. Why do you think the union doesn't want people to work more than two hours overtime?
6. Do you know anyone who does not have a job? What do they think about people who work a lot of overtime?
7. Did Chung Chi do the right thing? What would you do?

MUNG'S STORY: Mung works in a restaurant. Sometimes she works twelve hours a day, six days a week. She gets regular pay and tips, but she does not get overtime pay. She does not ask for it because she is afraid she will lose her job. She has many friends who do not have a job. She is just glad to have a job.

What should Mung do? Rank these solutions from best to worst (1 to 6); then in small groups, discuss your choices. Choose a group solution and explain it to the class.

1. Nothing.
2. She should ask for overtime pay.
3. She should quit and look for another job.
4. She should get a lawyer.
5. She should refuse to work overtime.
6. Other (add your own solution) _____

ACTION ACTIVITIES

A. COMPETENCY: Figuring out overtime pay

HOURLY RATE: Hourly workers' overtime rate is one and a half (1.5) times their regular rate of pay. Look at this example of figuring out overtime pay:

> Your hourly wage: $6.00
> Number of hours worked in one week: 48
> Overtime rate: 1.5 × $6, or $9.00 per hour
> Number of hours overtime: 8 (48 – 40)
> Total overtime pay: 8 × $9 = $72
> Regular pay: 40 × $6 = $240
> Total pay: $240 (regular pay) + $72 (overtime pay) = $312

PIECE RATE: There are two ways employers can figure overtime pay for piece workers. They can divide the total weekly earnings by the total number of hours worked in the week. The worker gets half of this rate for each hour over 40 plus the full piecework earnings.

> Number of hours worked in one week: 45
> Total earnings for the week: $252
> Regular rate: $252 divided by 45, or $5.60 per hour
> Overtime premium: .5 × $5.60 = $2.80
> Number of hours overtime: 5 (45 – 40)
> Total overtime pay: 5 × $2.80 or $14
> Total pay: $252 (regular pay) + $14 (overtime pay) = $266

Another way to figure out overtime pay for piece workers is to pay 1.5 times the piece rate for each piece produced during overtime hours.

EXERCISE: Figure out your overtime pay for a week that you worked ten extra hours:

Hourly Workers		Piece Workers	
your hourly rate:	_____	number of hours worked:	_____
number of hours worked:	50	total earnings:	_____
overtime rate:	_____	regular rate:	_____
number of hours overtime:	_____	overtime premium:	_____
total overtime pay:	_____	number of hours overtime:	_____
regular pay:	_____	total overtime pay:	_____
total pay:	_____	total pay:	_____

B. COMPETENCY: Refusing overtime

Sometimes you may not want to work overtime. If overtime is *optional*, you can refuse to work. Add to these ways of *politely refusing overtime* and *giving your reason*.

Polite refusals	Reason/excuse
I would rather not stay.	I have to pick up my kids.
I'm sorry, but I can't.	I don't have a ride.

Caution: Before you refuse overtime, think about these questions: What will happen if you refuse? Will you get in trouble? Will you lose the chance for overtime another day?

ROLE PLAY: Practice conversations between a supervisor and a worker using these excuses:

1. Your daughter is sick.
        Example: Supervisor: Can you stay late tonight? We need to finish this job.
               Worker: I'm sorry, but I have to leave. My daughter is sick. But I'll work tomorrow if she's better.
2. Your supervisor needs four people to work late but you don't have child care.
3. Your supervisor wants you to stay late for the fifth night but you feel like you're getting sick.
4. (Add your own.) _____

STUDENT ACTION RESEARCH

INTERVIEWS: Find out overtime rules for your workplace or a friend's workplace. Add to this list of questions:

1. Do you have overtime in your workplace?
2. Are you covered by overtime laws? (See pages 67-68.)
3. Do you have to work overtime? Is it mandatory?
4. Can you refuse overtime? What happens if you do?
5. How many hours overtime can you work in one day?
6. How many days in a row can you work?

7. How many Saturdays in a row can you work?
8. Do you get paid for more than eight hours in one day?
9. Do you get overtime pay for working on holidays or weekends?
10. Have you ever had problems with overtime?

CODE WRITING: Write a code about a common overtime problem (see page 59 for more information about code writing). Make up questions for discussion of the code. Discuss possible solutions to the problem. Work on competencies you need to solve the problem.

READING: Voices from History

Throughout the book there are "Voices from History." These readings are by real workers or reporters who lived in the past. After you read each passage, discuss these questions:

1. When did this take place?
2. What happened? What is this worker/reporter talking about?
3. How are things the same or different today?
4. Why do you think things changed? How did the changes happen? What did people have to do to make the changes?

Life in the Shop
by Clara Lemlich

First let me tell you something about the way we work and what we are paid. There are two kinds of work—regular, that is salary work, and piecework. The regular work pays about $6 a week and the girls have to be at their machines at 7 o'clock in the morning and they stay at them until 8 o'clock at night, with just one-half hour for lunch in that time.

The shops. Well, there is just one row of machines that the daylight ever gets to—that is the front row, nearest the window. The girls at all the other rows of machines back in the shops have to work by gaslight, by day as well as by night. Oh, yes, the shops keep the work going at night, too.

The bosses in the shops are hardly what you would call educated men, and the girls to them are part of the machines they are running. They yell at the girls and they "call them down" even worse than I imagine the Negro slaves were in the South.

There are no dressing rooms for the girls in the shops. They have to hang up their hats and coats—such as they are—on hooks along the walls. Sometimes a girl has a new hat. It never is much to look at because it never costs more than 50 cents, but it's pretty sure to be spoiled after it's been at the shop.

We're human, all of us girls, and we're young. We like new hats as well as any other young women. Why shouldn't we? And if one of us gets a new one, even if it hasn't cost more than 50 cents, that means that we have gone for weeks on two-cent lunches—dry cake and nothing else.

The shops are unsanitary—that's the word that is generally used, but there ought to be a worse one used. Whenever we tear or damage any of the goods we sew on, or whenever it is found damaged after we are through with it, whether we have done it or not, we are charged for the piece and sometimes for a whole yard of the material.

At the beginning of every slow season, $2 is deducted from our salaries. We have never been able to find out what this is for.

from *New York Evening Journal,*
November 28, 1909

Getting Through the Day

Lesson 1   Rules and Responsibilities

CODE

Signs in illustration: NO SMOKING · NO TALKING · NO EATING OR DRINKING · NO MUSIC

Questions for discussion:

1. Where are these women? What are they doing?
Who is the man? What is his job?
What is he doing?
What are some of the rules in this workplace?

2. How do the women feel? What do you think they are thinking?
How does the man feel?
Should the workers smoke? Why or why not?
Should the supervisor smoke? Why or why not?

3. In your country, what were some of the work rules? What happened
    if you broke them?
What are some of the rules at your job here? What happens if you
    break them?
Do supervisors have rules at your job? What happens if they break them?
Have you ever gotten in trouble for breaking a rule? What rule did you
    break? What happened? Was it *fair* or *unfair*?

4. Why are there rules at work?
Why are there NO TALKING rules?
How do the rules help workers? How do rules help employers?
Does everyone have to follow the same rules?
What are some rules for management?
5. What can you do if you break a rule?
What can you do if a supervisor breaks a rule?

THINKING ACTIVITIES

A. RULES AND RESPONSIBILITIES FOR WORKERS

Here are some work rules and responsibilities. Discuss them with the others in your class. What do they mean? Which are true for all jobs? Which are true for your job? What is the reason for each rule? Do you think each is fair or unfair?

	All jobs	Your job
No talking on the job.	___	___
No horseplay.	___	___
No eating on the job.	___	___
No drinking on the job.	___	___
No swearing on the job.	___	___
No smoking.	___	___
No reading on the job.	___	___
No music or radios on the job.	___	___
No fighting.	___	___
No stealing.	___	___
You must be on time for work.	___	___
You must punch in.	___	___
No one else can punch in or out for you.	___	___
You must work carefully and well.	___	___
You must stay in your work area.	___	___
You must call in if you miss work.	___	___
You may not take tools home.	___	___
You must wear safety equipment.	___	___
You must wear a hair net.	___	___
You must wear your badge.	___	___
Others _____	___	___

B. READING: Hao's story

Read Hao's story; then discuss the italicized words and answer the questions.

Hao had a cold. He *called in* sick and talked to his supervisor. His supervisor asked, "When will you be back to work?" Hao said, "Probably in two days." Hao was sick for the whole week. When he came back to work, his supervisor told him he was terminated because he did not call in sick every day. He said, "If you miss three days without calling in, it is a *voluntary quit.*"

1. What did Hao say when he called in sick?
2. What rule did Hao break?
3. What happened to Hao?
4. Why do you think Hao did not call in every day?
5. What do you think Hao should do now?
6. Do you have a similar rule at your job?

ACTION ACTIVITIES

A. COMPETENCY: Calling in sick

At each job, the way to call in sick is different: sometimes you tell the person who answers the phone, sometimes you ask for personnel or your supervisor. Who do you tell at your job?

   Act out this conversation. Then find the lines where Mei-zhu did each of the following: *asking for someone, giving her name, her reason for calling, her excuse,* and *telling when she'll be back:*

Switchboard: Boston City Hospital.

Mei-zhu: Dietary, please.

Switchboard: Just a moment, please.

Supervisor: Dietary.

Mei-zhu: Hello, Sheila?

Supervisor: Yes.

Mei-zhu: This is Mei-zhu. I can't come in today.

Supervisor: What's wrong?

Mei-zhu: I'm sick. I have a fever.

Supervisor: That's too bad. When do you think you'll be back?

Mei-zhu: I should be better tomorrow or Thursday.

Supervisor: Call me if you're not.

Add to these lists of ways to call in sick:

Switchboard:	You:
Boston City Hospital.	*Asking for someone* Housekeeping, please. Sheila Watson, please.

	Giving your name and reason for calling
	This is _____ . I'm calling in sick.
	                I won't be coming in today.
	                I won't be in today.

Supervisor What's the problem?	*Giving your excuse* I have a fever. My daughter is very sick.
When will you be in?	*Telling when you'll be back* Tomorrow, I hope. I'm not sure, but I'll call.

PRACTICE: In pairs, practice calling in sick with each of these excuses:

1. You sprained your ankle.

2. You had car trouble.

3. Your daughter is sick.

4. You have a stomach flu.

5. Other: _____

B. COMPETENCY: Responding to discipline or reprimands

Act out this conversation. Then find where the worker *apologizes* and *gives an excuse.*

Supervisor: Anna, you're late again.

Anna: I'm sorry. I had a problem with my babysitter.

Supervisor: You better do something about her. If you're late again, I'm putting you on notice.

Anna: I'm looking for another babysitter.

Add to these lists of ways to respond to discipline:

Apology	Explanation or excuse
I'm sorry.	I didn't see the sign.
Sorry.	I didn't know that.
	I had trouble with _____

PRACTICE: With a partner, act out dialogues for responding to these reprimands:

1. You didn't punch in. **4.** Where's your hair net?
2. You can't eat on the job. **5.** Why didn't you call in yesterday?
3. Please stop talking. **6.** You've been late twice this week.

If you get a warning or reprimand about problems with your work you can also *ask for help*.

> Example: Supervisor: You wired that board wrong again.
> Worker: I'm sorry. Where is my mistake?

Add to these lists of *excuses* and *requests for help*:

Excuses	Requests for help
I ran out of _____.	Could you show me what's wrong?
I can't find the problem.	Could you explain it again?

PRACTICE: Act out responding to these reprimands:

1. The bathroom in 502 is dirty.
2. You used the wrong part on that job.
3. You broke three dishes today.
4. Mrs. Jones in room 402 is complaining about her floor.

C. COMPETENCY: Responding to unfair discipline

Have you ever been disciplined for something you think is not fair? What did you do? Together, list all the things you can do if you are unfairly disciplined.

Read this dialogue. What do you think Manny should do? On a separate sheet of paper, rank the solutions, first individually and then in groups.

Supervisor: This is your fourth mistake today. You can leave for the day.
Manny: I'm sorry. My machine is broken; I reported it.
Supervisor: That's no excuse. You're responsible for your work.

He should: **1.** apologize, leave, and do nothing
2. get angry with his boss
3. ask for his union representative
4. quit and look for another job
5. get help from other workers
6. other _____

ROLE PLAY: Discuss the *consequences* of each choice: What will happen if you do nothing? What may happen if you get angry with your boss? If you ask other workers for help? If you ask for union help? Act out three different endings to the dialogue, including what Manny would say and the response he would probably get.

THINKING ACTIVITIES

A. IDENTIFYING EMPLOYERS' RESPONSIBILITIES

Workers are not the only ones who have to follow rules. There are federal laws about wages (Unit IV), safety conditions (Unit VI), discrimination (Unit VII), and many other aspects of work. Each state also has its own laws about working conditions. Here are some of the laws for Massachusetts:

The Right to a Seat: The employer must allow workers to sit while they are working *except* when the job cannot be done sitting down or when sitting would be dangerous.

Restrooms: The employer must provide clean bathrooms, with good light, towels, soap, and paper.

In unionized workplaces, there are also union rules for employers. Here are some examples of union rules:

1. Supervisors cannot work on the assembly line.
2. Supervisors must give warnings before suspending someone.
3. The employer must provide safety gloves.

B. RESPONDING TO EMPLOYER VIOLATIONS

Raoul just got an inspector's job at his factory. He waited a long time to get into a higher job classification. The new job pays more than the old one and it is easier. But every time someone is sick, the foreman puts Raoul back on his old job. This is against union regulations.

1. Make a class list of all the things Raoul could do.
2. Discuss the consequences of each choice: Is it safe for Raoul? Is it effective? Will he stop the rule violation?
3. Rank the choices from best to worst. Discuss your choices in small groups until you get a group solution.

ACTION ACTIVITIES

A. COMPETENCY: Requesting advice

Sometimes you may not know what to do if the employer is breaking a rule. You may want to ask another worker's advice. Add to this list of how to ask for advice:

State the problem	Ask advice
Mr. Lee wants me to do Jo's job.	What should I do?
They won't give us any soap.	What can we do?

PRACTICE: In pairs, act out a dialogue between two workers about these problems. One worker should ask for advice; the other should suggest a solution and give reasons.

1. The boss is smoking in a no-smoking area.
2. You have no heat in your work area.
3. The boss tells you to work through lunch.
4. The boss is working on the assembly line.
5. (Add your own.) _____

B. COMPETENCY: Filing a grievance

If you are in a union, you can file *grievances* about problems that are covered in your union contract. A grievance is a written complaint. Act out this dialogue. Then practice filing grievances for the problems in the preceding *Practice* section.

Juan: I need some gloves.
Supervisor: I'll get them later.
Juan: But I need them now. This stuff is dangerous.
Supervisor: Just work carefully.
Juan: I'd like to talk to my committeeman.

Committeeman: What's the problem?
Juan: I can't get safety gloves. I want to file a grievance.
Committeeman: Did you ask your foreman?
Juan: Yes. He said to work without them.
Committeeman: What's your name and badge number?

READING: Rights to organize for change as a group

Sometimes it is dangerous or difficult to make changes alone. Groups of workers who try to make changes together have legal protections. Divide into groups. Each group should read one question about group actions, discuss it, and report about it to the class.

1. What does the National Labor Relations Act (NLRA) say? You have the right to organize *with other workers* to change your wages, hours, and working conditions. Two or more employees are protected if they try to improve working conditions or take action to benefit more than one employee. This law only covers *concerted* action—action by two or more employees.

2. Who is covered by the NLRA? People who work for private companies are usually covered. The Act does not cover railroads and airlines, and small businesses (with less than $500,000 revenue). State laws may cover other workers.

3. What can two or more workers do under the NLRA? They can:

—Meet together to discuss wages or other workplace issues with each other before and after work and during breaks
—Complain to management about workplace conditions
—Make demands for better working conditions or wages
—Object to the firing or transfer of another worker
—Write letters or petitions asking for changes
—Request meetings to discuss work problems
—Pass out leaflets about working conditions (but not during work)

4. What happens if an employer tries to punish you for these activities? It is illegal to harass, transfer, discipline, or fire employees who take part in group action for change. If an employer violates the NLRA, it is called an *unfair labor practice.* You must file a complaint with the National Labor Relations Board (NLRB) within six months of the violation. There will be a *hearing* to see who is right. The employer may have to rehire a worker with back pay and interest. However, it often takes a long time for the NLRB to act on complaints.

Example: Carol Rotman, a photocopy machine operator in a printing company, got together with some of her co-workers to talk about how the air conditioning didn't work. When she complained to the owner, he got angry and fired her. The firing is illegal because she was acting with a group of others to improve conditions. If she files a complaint with the NLRB, it can order the company to give her job back to her with back pay, interest, and benefits.

STUDENT ACTION RESEARCH

1. Find out the rules for employees at your job. Ask another worker to get a list of rules from personnel. Bring it to class and discuss it with other students.

2. Make up questions like these about employers' responsibilities in your state and in your workplace:

Do employers have to provide safety gloves?
Do employers have to provide first aid rooms?
Do employers have to provide telephones?
Do employers have to provide coffee machines?
Can supervisors do your work?
Can employers suspend you with no warning?

With your teacher, discuss how to find answers to these questions. Invite a labor lawyer, a union representative, or an advocate for immigrant workers to class. Begin to make a list like this of agencies in your city that can help with work questions and problems.

Agency	Contact person	Phone

3. Compare rules for employees and rules for employers. Make a chart like this:

Employees have to	Employers have to
call in every day	let us sit down

Employees cannot	Employers cannot
talk at work	make us work through lunch

LOG: Write a story about a time when you or a friend of yours broke a rule or was disciplined at work. What happened? What did the employer do? How did you or your friend respond?

CODE WRITING: Write a code about a time when a supervisor violated a rule at work. Make up questions to go with it.

INTERVIEWS: Ask an American worker these questions: Have you ever tried to change anything with a group of co-workers? What was the problem? What did you do? What happened?

Lesson 2 The Deportation Scare

CODE

Pierre: It seems like this line is getting faster and faster.

Jean: I know. But what can we do?

Pierre: Maybe we should all get together and complain.

Jean: Are you kidding? They'll get rid of us in a minute. Or they'll call in Immigration to check our papers. You don't want to be sent back to Haiti, do you?

Pierre: My papers are OK. I have a green card. But I guess you're right. Not everyone here has papers.

Jean: Besides, it's not our country. We shouldn't say anything. I'm just lucky to have a job.

Questions for discussion:

1. What is the problem in this factory?
What does Pierre want to do about it?
What does Jean say about his ideas?
What might the company do?

2. Do you think Pierre and Jean are here legally?
How does Pierre feel? How does Jean feel? Why?
Why does Pierre decide not to complain?
What does *deportation* mean?

3. Did you ever have a speed-up at work? What happened?
Did the workers do anything about it? Why or why not?
Did you ever work anywhere where workers were deported?
     What happened?
Do you ever feel like a guest in this country?

4. Why do you think illegal workers come to this country?
Why do you think employers hire them?
What are some of the problems of *undocumented* workers?
What are the fears of workers *with* green cards?
Do you think non-Americans should keep quiet and be thankful for any job
     (as Pierre says)?

5. Do you think Pierre and Jean should do anything about their problem
     by themselves? With other workers? What should they do?
Can undocumented workers do anything about work problems?
What can they do? How can they do it?

READING: Legal Information about deportation

Divide into groups. Each group should read one or two questions and report on it to the rest of the class.

1. Can the government deport documented workers (with green cards)? In the story, Pierre had his green card. But he was afraid of being sent back to Haiti. In fact, the main reasons aliens can be sent back are:

- —if they leave the U.S. for a long period of time.
- —if they commit crimes.
- —if they gave false information when they got their green cards.
- —if they belong to "subversive" organizations (organizations which act against the government).

Sometimes an employer will call the Immigration and Naturalization Service (INS) if foreign-born workers are organizing for better conditions or a union. This is a way to scare workers. If the INS does come to a workplace, foreign-born workers still have some rights.

2. Can government agents search or arrest anyone who looks foreign whenever they want to? No, government agents must have a good reason to think you have no papers if they arrest or search you. For example, Puerto Ricans are American citizens and do not have green cards. It is illegal for INS agents to arrest them just because they look Spanish. ALIENS HAVE THE RIGHT TO BE FREE FROM UNREASONABLE SEARCH AND ARREST.

3. What should you do if INS agents stop you? The first thing you should do is ask if they have a warrant allowing them to stop you. Then you can ask for a lawyer. You do not have to answer any questions without a lawyer.

You have the right to remain silent. You cannot be deported for being silent.

You have the right to be free from threats and coercion. Sometimes, INS agents may try to scare you. They may say you will be deported or put in jail if you do not answer questions. Sometimes they may even try to physically force you to answer questions. You do not have to answer questions if they try to hurt or scare you.

You have the right to a lawyer. You can have a lawyer that you choose and pay for. The government does not have to appoint a lawyer to defend you if you cannot pay. If you ask for a lawyer, the INS agents MUST stop asking you questions until the lawyer is there.

4. Can the INS keep you locked up without a hearing? The INS can let you go on bond (you pay an amount of money set by the court) or keep you locked up. If you do not agree with their decision, you have the right to ask the immigration judge to decide.

5. Can INS agents go to your home and search it? You DO NOT HAVE TO tell the INS where you live or let them into your home. YOU HAVE THE RIGHT TO BE FREE FROM SEARCH OF YOUR PERSON OR HOME. INS agents do not have the right to search your home without your permission or an order from the court.

GRAMMAR: Modals (cannot, must, have to, should)

For each of these questions about deportation raids, give three possible answers:

1. What are three things the INS cannot do?

Example: The INS cannot try to hurt you.

The INS _____.

2. What are three things the INS must do?
3. What are three things you do not have to do?
4. What are three things you should do?

FINDING RESOURCES

If you think you may have trouble with the INS, it is a good idea to carry a lawyer's telephone number with you. Do you know the name of a lawyer who speaks your language? Are you sure this lawyer will give you good advice? Do you have recommendations for this lawyer?

Lawyer's name: _____

Lawyer's phone number: _____

ACTION ACTIVITIES

COMPETENCY: Asking for a lawyer

Act out the following dialogue. Show where Juan *explains his problem, asks for a lawyer,* and *insists on his rights.*

INS: Can you show me your green card?
Juan: I don't have my papers here.
INS: Then you should come with me.
Juan: But my papers are at home.
INS: I'm sorry. You're coming with us. We need to ask you some questions.
Juan: I'd like to call my lawyer.
INS: Where do you live?
Juan: I'll answer your questions when my lawyer is here.

Add to these lists:

Explaining the problem
I am from Puerto Rico. I don't have a green card.
My papers are at home.

Asking for a lawyer
May I call my lawyer?
I need to call my lawyer.

Add to these lists of ways to insist on your rights:

Insisting on a lawyer (the right to a lawyer)
I have the right to call my lawyer.
I won't answer until my lawyer is here.

Refusing to answer questions (the right to remain silent)
I don't have to answer that.

Rejecting threats (the right to be free from threats)
You have no right to threaten me.
It's illegal to threaten me.

Refusing to let someone in your home (the right to be free from search)
You can't come in my house.
I'm sorry, but I don't have to let you in.

ROLE PLAY: The INS hears that there are undocumented workers in a laundry. One student plays the part of a worker who is Puerto Rican (a U.S. citizen). Another is the INS agent. A third student is an undocumented worker. The INS agent tells the Puerto Rican he will be sent home if he doesn't give his address. The INS worker tells them both that they must answer questions or they will be sent to jail. What does each person say or do in this situation?

READING: Interview with an undocumented worker

Pedro is from South America. This is his real story, but it is not his real name. Read this interview and then make up questions about it for each other.

Question: Why did you come to the United States?

Pedro: There were three government changes in four months. I worked for a civilian government in the capital as an accountant. When the military took over, I was fired. I had no money and couldn't get a job. My wife and I, at first, were only going to visit my parents in the U.S., but after the coups I realized I had to stay here.

Question: How did you get your first job in Boston?

Pedro: A friend from my country worked in a restaurant and got me a job there. I had been here about two months. It was work I had never done before . . . I was paid only $3.15 an hour, with no lunch break. I quit after four months.

Question: Where do you work now?

Pedro: I have worked in one of Boston's hotels for the past three years. This place is better and I have learned the work and am good at it.

Question: Are there many undocumented workers there?

Pedro: I don't know. We don't ask because we don't want to scare or embarrass each other. Among the Hispanics, we talk and gradually become friends, but we never ask about green cards. . . .

Question: Are you afraid to complain or speak up because of having no papers?

Pedro: Many people are. Especially people who are alone or can't go home for political reasons. They can't take chances. But I never feared complaining. I feel you have to defend yourself. But it is dangerous. I had two friends picked up by Immigration because, I believe, a superior they were fighting with reported them.

Lesson 3 Stress

CODE

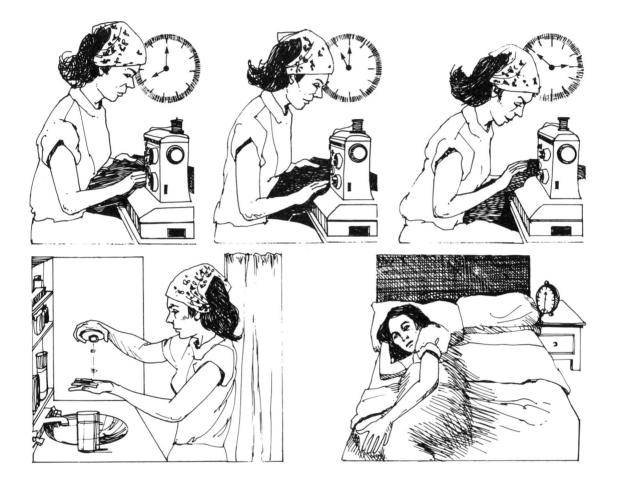

Teacher: Is something wrong, Maria? You've been missing a lot of classes.

Maria: I always have headaches after work.

Teacher: Have you been to a doctor? Maybe you need glasses.

Maria: He says there's nothing wrong with me. But I feel like I'm going crazy. I can't sleep and I'm always nervous.

Questions for discussion:

1. How does Maria feel after work?
Does she feel this way often?
What did the doctor say to her? Does she need glasses?
What other problems does she talk about?
2. Do you think Maria is sick?
Why do you think she has headaches and trouble sleeping?
3. Do you ever feel like Maria?
When do you get headaches?
Do you often have other problems like tired eyes, frequent colds, or
   stomach problems?
4. Why do you think you have these problems?
What is *stress*? How does stress make you feel?
What are some reasons people feel stress?
5. What are some things you can do about stress?

This lesson looks at three questions:

1. What are the *signs* of stress?
2. What are the *causes* of stress? Why do you feel stress?
3. What are the *remedies*? What can you do about stress?

THINKING ACTIVITIES: Signs or symptoms of stress
IDENTIFYING SYMPTOMS OF STRESS

Here are some health problems that may be caused by stress. They are
physical signs or symptoms of stress. Discuss their meanings and make
up questions about each symptom. Use these questions to interview your
teacher and each other.

> Example: <u>Sign</u>
>
> headaches
> insomnia
> tired eyes
>
> <u>Question</u>
>
> Do you have headaches very often?
> Do you have trouble sleeping?
> Do your eyes bother you?

Make a list of all the signs of stress in your class.

a. headaches
b. insomnia
c. tired eyes and blurred vision
d. frequent colds or other sickness (lowered resistance)
e. stomach problems: diarrhea, change of appetite, ulcers
f. heart problems: high blood pressure, heart attacks
g. toothaches (from tension in your jaws and grinding teeth)
h. depression, nervousness, anger
i. unusual tiredness
j. nervous twitches
k. sexual problems

THINKING ACTIVITIES: Causes of stress

A. IDENTIFYING CAUSES OF STRESS

Stress may come from many places: problems with working conditions, time, people at work, and family. Discuss these causes of stress and match them with the sentences below:

a. too much noise (even noise that doesn't damage hearing)
b. uncomfortable seating
c. poor lighting
d. time problems: not enough break time, too much overtime, speed-ups, shift changes, sitting or standing in one place for a long time
e. repetitive work: doing the same thing over and over
f. temperature problems: hot or cold areas, temperature changes
g. worry about chemicals
h. worry about dangerous equipment
I. problems with supervisors
J. problems with other workers
k. worry about lay-offs or job security

_c_ **1.** The lights are too bright.
____ **2.** We only have one five-minute break
____ **3.** We have to work very fast.
____ **4.** The machines are very loud.
____ **5.** I bend over a table all day.
____ **6.** I work different shifts every week.
____ **7.** I'm worried about getting burned by the hot glue.
____ **8.** The other workers take my work.
____ **9.** I'm standing up all day long.
____ **10.** I have to work 10 hours every day.
____ **11.** My supervisor gives me more work than anyone else.
____ **12.** I never know if I'll work a full week.
____ **13.** I go in and out of the cold storage room all the time.
____ **14.** I think the fumes are dangerous.

B. CLASS CHART

Make a chart like this, matching some of the signs of stress with their causes. Talk about what you can do *by yourself* about the problem. Then discuss different things you could do *with others*.

Signs	Causes	Remedies	
I feel	*because*	*What can I do?*	*What can we do?*
tired	I work so fast	ask for more breaks	
headaches	noise	wear earplugs	ask them to fix the machines
feet hurt	stand all day	do exercises	ask for seats

GRAMMAR PRACTICE (*because* clauses): Make sentences like these:

> I feel tired because I work so fast.
> I have headaches because of the noise.
> My feet hurt because I stand all day.

Verb conjugations: Make chants like this one about stress:

I've got a headache.	What am I gonna do?
You've got a headache.	What are you gonna do?
She's got a headache.	What's she gonna do?
We've all got headaches	What are we all gonna do?
Because there's so much noise.	Because of all this noise?

> (Make up a third verse with solutions.)

THINKING ACTIVITY: Remedies for stress

Joanna works in an area with poor lighting. She often has sore eyes and headaches after work; she is tired a lot. What do you think she should do? Add to these lists of possible remedies for stress. Rank the choices individually and then in small groups. Explain your solutions to the class.

AT WORK		AT HOME
by herself	*with others*	
1. do nothing	**1.** suggest changes in the lighting	**1.** sleep more
2. skip work	**2.** bring in lamps	**2.** drink to relax
3. complain to the boss		

ACTION ACTIVITIES: Remedies for stress

A. COMPETENCY: Requesting breaks

INTERVIEWS: One way to ease stress is to get away from the job for a short time. Most jobs include breaks or relief time. Interview another student about breaks at his or her job (or at a previous job). Add to this list of questions:

> What are breaks called at your job? (relief time? rest?)
> How many breaks do you have?
> How long are the breaks?
> Can you ask for extra breaks?
> What will happen if you ask for a break? How will your boss feel?
> How often do you ask for breaks?
> Do you have any problems with breaks?

You can ask for a break the same way you start any other request: use a *polite opener, make the request* and *give a reason.* Add to these lists:

Polite Opener	Request	Reason
Excuse me.	Could I take a break?	I don't feel well.
	Would you mind if I sit down?	I feel dizzy.

Add to these lists of responses you might get:

Positive answers	Wait	Negative answers
Go ahead.	In awhile.	I can't spare you now.
Make it quick.	I'll have to find	You'll have to wait
I guess so.	someone to cover for you	till lunch.

ROLE PLAY: Act out these three situations. Tape record your role plays. Listen to the tapes and discuss what each student did well. Discuss different ways to say the same things.

1. An assembly line worker wants to go to the bathroom. The foreman gets someone to do his job.
2. An assembly line worker wants to get some water. The foreman tells her to wait.
3. A restaurant worker wants to phone home. The boss tells him it's too busy and to keep working.

B. COMPETENCY: Suggesting changes

If you can identify a specific problem, sometimes you can ask for changes or make a suggestion. Act out the following dialogue and find the lines where Mario *states the cause of the stress, states the results,* and *makes a suggestion.*

Mario: Do you have a minute? We have a problem.

Foreman: What is it?

Mario: There isn't enough light. We all have tired eyes and headaches. It's hard to do our work.

Foreman: Electricity costs money.

Raoul: We could do a better job with more light. Could we make a suggestion?

Foreman: What is it?

Jose: Maybe you could lower the light fixtures.

Foreman: I'll check into it.

Does this conversation sound real? What do you think would happen if you asked for a change at your job? Would it be better to ask by yourself or with other workers? Why?

Add to these lists of ways of suggesting changes:

Polite opener
Do you have a minute? We'd like to ask about something.
We have a problem. Is this a good time to talk about it?

State the PROBLEM OR THE CAUSE of the stress
There isn't enough light.
It's hard to work with so much noise.

State the RESULTS of the problem (how it affects your work)
We all have tired eyes and headaches.
It's hard to concentrate on our work.

Make a SUGGESTION
Could we make a suggestion? Maybe you could lower the lights.
We would work better with open windows.

Ask for TIME to try your plan
Could we try it for a week?

ROLE PLAY: In small groups, list ways to change each of the following situations. Choose the best solution, then act out a conversation with the supervisor suggesting changes.

1. You got moved to second shift and are worried about never seeing your children.
2. Noisy radiators give you and your co-workers headaches.
3. Three jobs were combined into two. You can't keep up and are missing parts of the job.

C. COMPETENCY: Reducing stress outside work

INTERVIEWS: It is not always possible to make changes at work. Look at the following list of things you can do about stress outside work. Add to the list and make questions from it; interview each other about ways of dealing with stress. Report back to class about the most helpful ways of relieving stress.

Do you do this?   Does it help?

Get enough sleep. (Do you get enough sleep?)
Drink alcohol.
Talk to friends.
Get exercise.
Play sports.
Watch T.V.
Cry.

Other _____

TIME MANAGEMENT: Make a chart of your day. What do you do with your time?

Activity	Number of hours	Where does your time go?
work	_____	(Divide the circle into pieces. Each piece represents the amount of time you spend on a certain activity. This kind of graph is called a *pie graph*.)
shopping	_____	
cooking	_____	
cleaning	_____	
child care	_____	
relaxing	_____	
exercise	_____	
friends	_____	
sleeping	_____	
other	_____	

DISCUSSION:

1. What activities do you spend a lot of time on?
2. What do you spend a little time on?
3. What activities could you spend *less* time on?
4. What activities could you spend *more* time on?
5. Where in your day could you find more time for relaxing or getting exercise?

RELAXATION EXERCISE: Try this exercise together.

1. Find a point about eight to ten feet in front of you. Stare at it. Try to think of nothing for about 30 seconds.
2. Sit up straight. Close your eyes and tighten your eye muscles hard. Now slowly relax and open your eyes. Breathe in through your nose and out through your mouth.
3. Bite your teeth together hard and then slowly relax.
4. Tighten your shoulders; then relax. Do the same for your arms, then your stomach, your thighs, hips, calves, feet.
5. Tighten your whole body; relax. Be quiet for one minute. Open your eyes.

STUDENT ACTION RESEARCH

INTERVIEWS: Do other people at your workplace complain about headaches, sore eyes, or health problems? Make a list of questions for your co-workers about *symptoms* of stress (from page 85). Make another list of questions about possible *causes* of stress.

What might happen if you asked these questions? What could you say to explain your reasons for asking them? If you feel comfortable about it, interview some co-workers about symptoms and causes of stress.

CHART: Make a chart like this that matches symptoms and causes of stress for your workplace:

Symptoms	Causes
sore back	poor headaches
insomnia	worry about lay-offs

FINDING REMEDIES: Look at your charts. Is it possible to get rid of all the causes of stress? Is there *one* problem that could be changed? Discuss these questions to find a remedy:

1. What is the cause of the problem?
2. What are some possible remedies? Which is the best?
3. Who could help you in asking for a change?
4. What could you say?
5. What might the response be?

ROLE PLAY: Act out suggesting a change. Act out different ways your supervisor might respond. Practice what you would do in your workplace to make the change.

ACTION: Decide if you want to try suggesting a change at your job. Report back what happens.

Acting for Health and Safety

Lesson 1   A Safe Workplace

CODE

Supervisor: What happened?

Alex: Mario burned his arm.

Supervisor: Again? You people have to work more carefully. You're not paying attention to your jobs.

Alex: It's the fumes. They make us dizzy.

Supervisor: That's no excuse. Mario was probably careless. There are too many accidents in this department.

Alex: It's not Mario's fault. We can't breathe in here. There's no air.

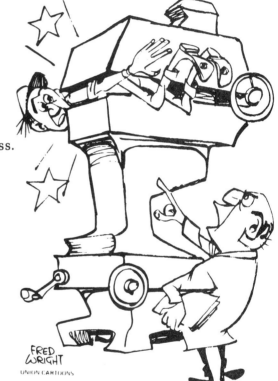

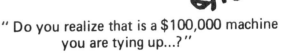

FRED WRIGHT
UNION CARTOONS

" Do you realize that is a $100,000 machine you are tying up...?"

Questions for discussion:

1. What happened to Mario?
Is this his first accident?
Who is Alex?

2. Has anyone else had an accident in this department?
Why did Mario burn his arm? What does Alex think?
   What does his supervisor think?
What problem do the workers have?

3. Have you ever had an accident at work?
Why did it happen? Were you careless?
Whose fault was it?
What did you do? What did your employer do?

4. Do you think Mario was careless?
Do you think the supervisor or the company was careless?
Who was responsible?
Do you think most accidents are caused by careless workers? Why?
Do you think most accidents are caused by careless employers? Why?

5. What should the workers in this story do?
What do they need to know to do this?
What are the safety responsibilities of workers?
What are the safety responsibilities of employers?

THINKING ACTIVITIES

A. ATTITUDES ABOUT HEALTH AND SAFETY AT WORK

Read each sentence (ask about any sentence you don't understand). First, check *agree* or *disagree* for each. Then discuss your answers in small groups and find a group opinion. Report your group opinions to the class with reasons.

	Your opinion	Group opinion
	AGREE/DISAGREE	AGREE/DISAGREE
1. Most accidents happen at work because workers are careless.	___ ___	___ ___
2. If a worker tries to improve safety at work, he/she may get in trouble.	___ ___	___ ___
3. Management knows that "safety pays" and will take care of safety problems.	___ ___	___ ___
4. There are always safety problems at a job; you just have to accept them.	___ ___	___ ___
5. If you worry about safety you will go crazy; let the union or the employer worry about it.	___ ___	___ ___

B. VOCABULARY

Read these sentences. Try to figure out the meaning of the italicized words, using the rest of the sentence, the next sentence, or your experience. Explain each sentence in your own words.

1. Any job can have *hazards*. There may be dangerous *substances* or *conditions* on your job. Substances can include paints, glues, chemicals, dust. Conditions can include broken machines, wet floors, heat, noise, *vibration*, and *radiation*.
2. Scientists don't know the safe *level of exposure* to many substances. They don't know how much *contact* is safe. In addition, substances *affect* people differently.
3. Sometimes there are *delayed effects*. Illness may not appear for a long time after contact with the substance.
4. Substances can get into your body different ways: you can *inhale* substances through your mouth or nose; you can *absorb* them through your skin; or you can *swallow* them through your mouth.

C. WORKERS' RESPONSIBILITIES

GRAMMAR: Modals (might, could) Each workplace has its own safety rules that workers are expected to follow. Here are some of them. Write down the reason for each rule (the first two are done for you). Which of these rules do you have in your workplace?

1. Rule: Don't wear loose clothes around machines.
   Reason: They *might* get caught in a machine.
2. Rule: Wear strong shoes. Don't wear sandals.
   Reason: You *could* hurt your feet. A box could fall on your toes.
3. Rule: Tie back long hair; don't wear hair loose near machines.
4. Rule: Wear hair nets when working with food.
5. Rule: Don't wear jewelry (earrings, necklaces, etc.) around machinery.
6. Rule: Wear work gloves around chemicals.
7. Rule: Wear safety glasses or goggles.
8. Rule: Wear ear plugs or earmuffs in noisy areas.
9. Rule: Wear a mask or respirator around dust or fumes.
10. Rule: Wear a hard hat in areas where things may fall.
11. Rule: Keep your work area clean and neat. Don't leave anything on the floor.
12. Rule: Put tools and equipment away.
13. Rule: Clean up spills and leaks.
14. Rule: Bend your knees when you lift something heavy.
15. Rule: Know where exits and fire extinguishers are.
16. Rule: Don't leave your machine running while you're away.
17. Rule: Use the safety catch on your machine.
18. Rule: Obey safety signs. (Ask if you don't understand them.)
19. Rule: Report safety problems to your supervisor.
20. Rule: (Add your own.) _____

PRACTICE: What clothing rules do each of these workers need to follow?

1. hospital cafeteria worker: prepares food trays

   Example: She or he needs to wear a hair net, gloves, and a uniform.

2. auto spray painter: paint and chemicals in the air
3. rubber worker: chemicals in liquids and air
4. construction worker: around falling objects
5. drill operator: around noisy machinery
6. welder: sparks flying around
7. You: _____

PRACTICE: Read about the following accidents. What was the cause of the accident? What should the worker do next time?

1. New work was added to John's job. He had to work very fast to keep up. He cut his finger on one of the parts.
2. Maria usually lifted empty boxes. She lifted one heavy box and hurt her back.
3. Herb had to work overtime every night. One night he burned himself when he was very tired.
4. The safety catch was broken on Ann's machine. She told the supervisor. He said he would take care of it at lunch. She went back to work and got cut.
5. Luisa left a broom in a bucket in the hall of a nursing home. One of the patients tripped and fell.
6. (Add an accident from your job.) _____

READING: Employers' responsibilities

Keeping a workplace safe is not just the workers' job. In 1970, the Occupational Safety and Health Act (OSHA) was passed. This law says that employers must make sure that working conditions are safe. It says that *workers have the right to a safe and healthy workplace.*

Divide into small groups. Each group should read one question and report on it to the whole class.

1. What hazards do employers have to protect workers from?
Employers must make their workplace safe and free of health hazards "as far as possible." They must protect workers from:

—high noise levels that cause hearing or heart problems
—substances that cause cancer
—broken ladders, unguarded stairs, poor scaffolds
—poor ventilation of dust and fumes that can cause lung problems
—machinery that can cause injuries with no guards or emergency switches
—poor wiring or electrical problems
—poor equipment that can cause explosions, fires, crashes, or other accidents
—fumes that can cause kidney, nerve, liver problems

2. What do employers have to do to protect workers?
Employers must follow government safety and health standards. Over 5,000 standards say that employers must:

—provide guards and emergency switches on machinery
—keep safe levels of fumes, chemicals, dust, etc.
—keep equipment in good repair
—give workers safety clothes and equipment if necessary
—label chemicals if they are dangerous
—give workers regular medical check-ups if they work with dangerous materials (like lead or asbestos)
—give any information they have about toxic substances to workers who ask for it

3. What can OSHA do to make workplaces safer?
The Occupational Safety and Health Administration sets safety and health standards, inspects workplaces, orders employers to get rid of hazards, and fines employers who do not.

4. What can workers do to make their workplaces safer?
When OSHA first started, it caused many changes in workplace safety. Recently, OSHA has been less active. This means workers need to do more for their own safety. They need to learn to recognize workplace hazards, learn how to get information about hazards, report health or safety problems, file complaints with OSHA if necessary, and learn their safety rights.

Comprehension questions:

1. What are three things that employers must do to make their workplaces safe?

They must _____

They must _____

They must _____

2. What are three things that OSHA can do to make workplaces safe?

OSHA can _____

OSHA can _____

OSHA can _____

3. What are three things that workers should do to make their workplaces safe?

They should _____

They should _____

They should _____

STUDENT ACTION RESEARCH

WORKPLACE QUESTIONS: If you work, find out if there are any rules about clothing at your job. What clothing is required? Where do you get safety equipment or clothing? Who do you get it from? Does the employer pay for it? What do you do if there is no safety gear?

INTERVIEWS: Ask someone who has been at a job for a long time (either a friend or a co-worker) about a safety problem at work. What was the problem? Whose fault was it, or who caused the problem? What happened? What did the workers do? Was the problem solved?

Tape record your interviews; bring them to class and talk about the different ways that workers have dealt with unsafe conditions. What did they do? What worked? What did not work? What do you need to know to handle safety problems?

REALIA: Bring in any safety booklets or lists of rules from a workplace. Read the booklets and talk about their messages.

READING: Voices from History

The following report from a 1911 magazine shows how little immigrants' lives were valued. Here a journalist is talking to a railroad construction engineer; how are things the same or different today?

Health and Safety at the Turn of the Century

"To think," I exclaimed, "that not a man was killed."

"Who told you that?" asked the young assistant.

"Why, it's here in this report sent to the newspapers by your press agent. He makes a point of it."

The young assistant smiled. "Well, yes. I guess that's right," he replied. "There wasn't anyone killed except just wops."

"Except what?"

"Wops. Don't you know what wops are? Dagos, niggers, and Hungarians—the fellows that did the work. They don't know anything, and they don't count."

Lesson 2   Hazards in the Workplace

CODE

Robert: The report from the health and safety inspector is in.

Mary: What does it say?

George: It says there's no problem. The chemicals in the new paint finish are safe.

John: But we know there's a problem! We all have skin rashes on our hands!

George: The report says there's nothing wrong.

Mary: Well, we should know. We work here.

Questions for discussion:

1. Who is a health and safety inspector? What does he or she do?
   What health problem do the workers have?
   What do they think may be the reason for this problem?
   What does the health inspector's report say?
2. How do John and Mary feel about the health report?
   Do you think there is a health problem here?
3. Do any substances or conditions bother you at work?
   Have you ever had a health problem that someone said was *not* a problem?
     What happened? Who was right?
4. Why do you think the report says there is no problem?
   Who do you think is right—the workers or the health inspector? Who is
     the *expert* about health problems at work?
   Who benefits from this report?
5. What do you think the workers should do?
   Should they stop worrying about the skin rash?
   Should they try to do something about this problem? If so, what?
   What can you do if there's a health problem at your job?

THINKING ACTIVITIES

A. DECIDING TO FIND OUT ABOUT HAZARDS

Often workers are the real experts about conditions at their jobs. They may be the first to see or feel a problem. But feeling something is wrong is not always enough. To make a workplace safer and healthier, it is necessary to know what the hazards are and show that they are real.

Ask these questions about workplace conditions in pairs. If you answer *yes* to one or more of them, it may mean there's a hazard that you should find out about.

1. Do you often leave work with a headache or feeling sick?
2. Do you breathe chemicals or fumes all day?
3. Is there a bad smell at your workplace?
4. Is there so much noise that you need to shout to the person next to you?
5. Have there been many accidents on your machine or in your area?
6. Do lots of people at your job have the same health problem (headaches, skin problems, stomach problems, dizziness)?
7. Do people feel better on the weekends and get sick again on Monday?
8. Are people who have been on the job for many years very unhealthy?
9. Has your doctor ever asked you if you feel sick at work?

Make a class list of reasons some of you might want to find out more about hazards at your workplace:

> Example: Many people have back problems.
> There's a lot of dust and no ventilation.

B. CHART: Understanding what hazards are

Safety hazards are conditions that cause immediate harm, that is, accidents and injury (broken bones, cuts, loss of eyesight).

Health hazards are conditions that cause disease or illness (hearing loss, heart disease, cancer). They may come on slowly and be harder to distinguish.

Discuss new vocabulary in this chart and give examples of hazards from your own experience.

HEALTH HAZARDS

Stress	Physical	Chemical	Biological
speed-ups	noise	gases	contagious diseases
boring work	temperature	dusts	insects
repetitive work	dusts	cleaners	unclean conditions
supervisor-worker problems	vibration	acids	
worker-worker problems	radiation	metals (lead, mercury)	
	lifting	vapors/fumes	
	dampness	smoke	
	repetitive motion		

ACTION ACTIVITIES: Identifying hazards

How can you find out about hazards in your workplace? There are many research tools you can use:

1. Filling out a survey
2. Using your senses
3. Keeping written records about your work
4. Talking to other workers
5. Getting help from your employer, your union, OSHA, and other agencies

A. RESEARCH TOOL #1: Survey

Answer these questions about your workplace:

1. Do you have any safety problems because of the following:

____ housekeeping/clutter	____ machinery
____ electricity	____ poor safety equipment
____ fire	____ stairs, floors, exits
____ lifting	____ ladders
____ eye injuries	____ leaks, spills
____ trips and falls	____ other _____

2. Are there possible health hazards from the following:

____ toxic chemicals	____ temperature
____ dust	____ vibration
____ noise	____ poor lighting
____ infectious disease	____ other _____
____ radiation	

3. Have you or others had any of the following symptoms:

____ nausea, dizziness, or headaches

____ skin problems (rashes)

____ breathing problems (nose, throat problems)

____ frequent colds or unusual coughing

____ ringing ears, loss of hearing

____ aches and pains in chest, side, back

____ infections

____ childbirth problems or miscarriages

____ health problems that go away when you leave work

____ eye problems

____ problems worse than last year _____

B. RESEARCH TOOL #2: Using your senses

Your eyes, ears, and nose can pick out many safety hazards. Complete these
questions using *see*, *hear*, *feel*, and *smell*; answer them for your workplace:

Examples:

Can you see	broken stairs?
Can you hear	too much noise?
_____	dust in the air?
_____	dangerous machinery?
_____	flying sparks?
_____	bad wiring?
_____	some kinds of fumes?
_____	poor lighting?
_____	too much cold or heat?
_____	poor storage of boxes or equipment?
_____	too much vibration?

C. RESEARCH TOOL #3: Keeping records

You can also keep track of hazards with a written record. Look at this one:
What does it show? Why is it useful?

Date	Situation	Problem/Result
8/1/87	used new cleaner	skin rash
8/2–8/6	used old cleaner	no rash
8/7	used new cleaner	skin rash again

Is there any problem you might document with a record?

D. RESEARCH TOOL #4: Talking to other workers

If you have a skin rash, maybe other workers do. You can find out by
asking them.

Worker #1: I've had a rash since we started using this new cleaner. Have
you had any problems with it?

Worker #2: As a matter of fact, I have. I thought it was just me!

Worker #1: What do you think we should do?

Worker #2: Let's see if anyone else has the same problem.

In pairs, make up conversations like the one above about the following
problems:

1. headaches after work
2. losing hearing slowly
3. many illnesses from cold
4. backaches from hard benches

5. worrying about a chemical
6. dizziness from the heat
7. tired eyes from poor light
8. other _____

E. RESEARCH TOOL #5: Getting help and information

Divide into groups; each group should read one section and report about it to the class.

Sometimes you may need more information to solve a health or safety problem. For example, what are noise level standards? What chemicals are in the substances we use? Are they dangerous? You can get help and information in many places:

1. YOUR EMPLOYER: According to law, you have the *right to know* certain kinds of information about substances. Employers must give workers this information *if they have it.* Your employer must give you:

—your medical records.
—your exposure records (how much contact you've had with chemicals, radiation, noise, heat, etc.).
—information the employer already has about substances (safe levels of use, protections, effects of exposure).

2. UNION REPRESENTATIVES: If you're in a union, it can help you find out about substances and standards. It can:

—bring in its own experts to inspect the workplace.
—file grievances about health and safety problems.
—find out more information than individual workers can (according to the National Labor Relations Act).

If your local union is not able to help, you can call the Health and Safety Department of your international union.

3. OSHA OR OTHER AGENCIES: OSHA may send an inspector to your workplace to check on conditions. You may also be able to get help from NIOSH (National Institute for Occupational Safety and Health), from universities, and from COSH groups (state health and safety committees). *Note*: It often takes a long time to get results from these agencies.

4. WORKERS IN THE SUPPLY DEPARTMENT: Sometimes the names of chemicals or other substances are in or on the boxes that they come in. Shipping or supply workers may save these for you.

F. COMPETENCY: Asking for help or information

Act out this conversation. The safety rep is a union official who helps with health and safety problems. Find the lines where the worker *asks for help or information* and *states the problems.*

Worker: I have a question about noise in my area.
Safety Rep: What's the problem?
Worker: The machines are so loud that I have headaches. I told the boss— he told me to put cotton in my ears.
Safety Rep: There are OSHA standards about noise. I'll find out what they are and check your area.
Worker: What about ear plugs?
Safety Rep: OSHA says the company has to try to find ways to reduce the noise before making you use ear plugs. I'll see what they've done.
Worker: Thanks.

ROLE PLAY: Make up conversations where you ask about substances or standards for each of these cases. Whom would you ask? What would you say?

1. You work in an area with fumes. The company provides respirators, but they don't fit tightly and air gets in. You have asked your supervisor; he won't get new ones.
2. You are pregnant and work with a chemical that may be dangerous for pregnant women.
3. You have a skin rash. You think it comes from a new cleanser at work. You want to know what is in it.
4. (Add your own.) _____.

STUDENT ACTION RESEARCH

1. Make a hazards chart like this one for your workplace:

Hazard	How it affects us	What we can do
poor lighting	We all have sore eyes.	We should ask for more lights.
??????	We all have a skin rash.	We should find out what's in the new soap.

2. Find out the answers to these questions for your job:

Is there a safety committee? Who is on it?
Is there a company nurse? Will she help with health and safety problems?
Is there a union safety committee or representative?
What is the address and phone number of OSHA in your area?
What other occupational health and safety agencies are in your area?
Write down three numbers you could call for help with health and safety problems.

    1. _____

    2. _____

    3. _____

Lesson 3 Acting for Health and Safety

CODE

John: I'm not going back up there after lunch.

George: Why not?

John: There's something wrong with the scaffolding. I told the foreman, but he said it's OK. I don't think it's safe.

George: But you have to go. You'll get in trouble if you don't. They want the job done today.

John: I know. But what should I do? I don't want to lose my job, but I don't want to get hurt either.

Questions for discussion:

1. Where does John work?
   What is scaffolding?
   What is the problem with the scaffolding?
2. What is John worried about?
   What does George tell him?
   What did the foreman say?
   How does John feel after he talks to George?
3. Have you ever worked on a dangerous job?
   What did you do? What happened?
   In your country, what do workers do if a job is dangerous?

4. Why do employers sometimes ask workers to do unsafe jobs?
   Which do you think is more important—your job or your health?
5. What do you think John should do? What may happen if he goes back
   to work? What will happen if he doesn't?
   What were some of the ways you found that workers tried to change
   safety problems? (Interviews, Unit VI, Lesson 1)
   What ways worked best? What ways did not work?
   Is it easier to try to make changes alone or with others?

ACTION ACTIVITIES

A. COMPETENCY: Giving warnings

When something dangerous is about to happen, give a *warning* and a *reason*.

Warnings	Reasons
Watch out!	That's hot.
Look out!	The cart is moving.
Be careful!	The floor is slippery.
Hold it!	That's going to fall.
Stop!	Your shirt is caught.
Don't touch that!	It's wet.
Watch it!	There's a mop on the stairs

PRACTICE: Give warnings for these situations. Go around the room and
answer as quickly as possible.

1. Someone's hair is about to catch on fire.
2. Someone is about to touch hot metal.
3. Someone is about to step in a hole.
4. Someone is about to trip on a broom.
5. Someone is about to touch a dangerous chemical.
6. Someone is about to walk into the hospital room of someone with
   an infectious disease.
7. Someone is about to touch a sharp piece of metal.
8. Someone is about to touch a radio with wet hands.
9. Someone is about to light a match near gasoline.
10. Add your own (use *about to*). _____

B. COMPETENCY: Reporting a safety problem

When you have a safety problem at your job, whom do you tell? Do you tell
your supervisor, a safety representative, a co-worker, or someone else?

Read this conversation and find the lines where the worker *gets* Mr. Smith's
attention, reports the problem, states a possible result, and *makes a suggestion.*

Worker: Mr. Smith, there's a problem with my machine.
Mr. Smith: What is it?
Worker: The safety latch is broken. I'm afraid someone will get hurt. Could
you send someone to look at it?
Mr. Smith: Sure—as soon as I get a chance.
Worker: Thanks.

Add to this list of ways to report problems:

Get Attention

I think there's a safety problem in my department.
I'd like to report a safety problem.

Report the problem	State a possible result/reason
The safety catch is broken.	Someone could get cut.
There's water in the entry.	Someone may slip.
The fumes are making us dizzy.	The fan must be broken.

Make a suggestion

Could you send the repairman?
Could you get someone to clean it up?
I think we need a new fan.

ROLE PLAY: Finish this dialogue with both a positive response (Mr. Smith helps John) and a negative response (Mr. Smith doesn't help John).

John: Do you have a minute? I want to show you something.

Mr. Smith: What's up?

John: These respirators don't work. They let the dust in.

Positive responses	Negative responses
I'll send someone right over.	They're good enough. Don't worry about it.
I'll check into it.	That's OK. Go back to work.
I'll look into it.	That's no problem.
I'll take care of it.	
I'll get it fixed.	

Role play reporting each of these problems with both positive and negative responses from the supervisor. What would you say if the response was negative?

1. You have no safety gloves and must work with chemicals.
2. The fan is broken and you work with dangerous fumes.
3. The window is broken and it's 20 degrees outside.
4. There are many frayed wires in your work area.
5. (Add a problem from your experience.) _____.

C. COMPETENCY: Insisting on safety

What can you do if the employer doesn't want to change a safety problem? Here are some questions to think about before deciding what to do:

How serious is the problem?
What will happen if you do nothing?
Should you take action by yourself?
What may happen if you do?
Should you take action with others?
What may happen if you do?

Read these dialogues; find the lines where the workers *insist on safety*.

1. **Worker:** I need some gloves.

   Foreman: I don't have any today.

   Worker: Would you get some from another department? I can't work without them.

2. **Worker:** The fan isn't working. The fumes are making me dizzy.

   Foreman: I'll send someone after lunch.

   Worker: Could you send someone sooner? It's not safe.

ROLE PLAY: Act out what you would say or do in each of these situations.

1. You are pregnant and the fumes are making you sick. Your supervisor says the fumes are safe and he won't move you.

2. You work with twenty other people in an area where there is asbestos dust. Your respirators are not good and you can't get new ones.

READING: Filing a complaint with OSHA

Divide into groups; each group should report on one question.

1. What do OSHA regulations say? They say that you have the right to complain to management, OSHA, and the press about hazards on your job. You have the right to protest unsafe conditions even if you are not in a union.

> Example: A pregnant employee at a sewing company told her supervisor that glue fumes were making her sick. He said she was a "complainer" and fired her. She filed a charge with OSHA and got her job back with back pay.

> Example: A construction worker told a news reporter that he was working with asbestos dust. When the story came out in the paper, he was fired. He complained to OSHA and got back pay.

Note: The laws can't *stop* firings: they only help after you've been fired. It can take a long time to win.

2. Who can file a complaint? Any employee can file a complaint with OSHA. Unions, lawyers, family members of employees, and people who have left a job because of hazards can also file. Other people, like your doctor, can call OSHA to report a problem. OSHA will *not* tell your employer who filed if you don't want them to (see #4 and #5).

3. How do you file? OSHA has a form for complaints. It asks:

Where the hazard is located.

How many employees are exposed.

What injuries there have been.

What the employer knows about the hazard.

What the employer has done or not done.

4. What will OSHA do? If you sign the complaint and OSHA thinks there is a physical danger, an inspector will come to your workplace. If you do not sign the complaint, OSHA may just send the employer a letter about the complaint.

5. What will happen to you if you complain? You cannot be fired or punished for complaining about a health and safety problem. You can check the box "I do not want my name revealed to the employer" on the complaint form.

READING: Group action for health and safety

The law also protects workers who take direct action as a group (without going to OSHA). Two or more workers have the right to protest unsafe conditions (see Unit IV, Lesson 1). They have the right to use leaflets, petitions, picket lines, and press conferences before or after work; they should be careful not to hurt business with these activities. Divide into groups to read these stories. Make up questions about them.

1. A woman working at a bank in Boston was bothered by the noise from the printers in her work area. She and six co-workers discussed the problem. They came up with some good solutions. They met with their supervisor and made suggestions. At first, he stalled, but they kept insisting: finally the bank bought printer covers to reduce the noise.

2. When OSHA found high levels of lead in a chemical company, the workers decided not to eat in the lunch room (where there was lead). Instead they ate outside the company. They attracted the attention of the community and newspaper. The company quickly cleaned up the lead.

3. Workers at an assembly plant complained that a new fiberglass-coated wire was causing skin rashes. When the company did nothing, everyone with a skin problem visited the nurse. After 60 workers did this, the company changed the wire.

D. COMPETENCY: Refusing unsafe work

Sometimes you do not have time to wait for OSHA or other outside help. You may think that your life is in danger or a serious accident could happen at any moment. Under the OSHA law, you have the right to refuse unsafe work if *all* these things are true:

1. You have good reason to think that there is a real danger of death or serious injury.

2. You asked your supervisor to fix the problem and it was not fixed.

3. The danger is so urgent and immediate that there is no time to wait for an OSHA inspection.

4. You stay on the job and offer to work on something else.

5. There is no other choice.

> Example: At a company in Ohio, a net was put under an assembly line to catch falling parts. On June 28, 1974, George Cogwill was asked to clean the net. It broke when he got on it and he died. Twelve days later, two workers were told to clean the net. They suggested a way to clean it without walking on it, but their foreman didn't like the idea. The workers refused to climb on the net and were disciplined. They filed a complaint with OSHA and won. The U.S. Supreme Court said they had a right to refuse and ordered their records cleared.

PRACTICE: Look at each of these situations. Could you refuse to work? Why or why not?

1. A new chemical is giving you a rash. You tell your boss and he says he will look into it.
2. Someone's finger gets cut to the bone because the safety guard on his machine is broken. Your supervisor asks you to take his place. You ask him to fix the machine first. He says he can't because the whole line would stop.
3. The scaffolding on a construction job is broken. Your supervisor wants you to go on it anyway. He says he'll get it fixed after work. You're afraid it could break.
4. (Add a situation from *your* experience.) _____

Act out the following dialogue; find the lines where the worker *reports the problem, makes a suggestion,* and *refuses to work.*

John: I don't think we should work on the scaffolding.

Foreman: What's the problem?

John: The rope is loose and it's not safe.

Foreman: There's plenty of support. It'll be fine. We need to get this job done today.

John: Could you get someone to fix it before we go up?

Foreman: There's no time. Just get to work. Don't worry about it.

John: I'm sorry, but I'm not going up there until it's fixed. We could get killed.

Foreman: Then don't bother staying.

Add to these lists of ways of *reporting problems, making suggestions,* and *refusing to work:*

Report the problem	Make a suggestion
The ventilator doesn't work.	Could we stop until it's fixed?
The guard on the machine is broken.	Could you get it fixed?
The brakes on the truck need work.	Could I use another truck?

Refuse (only if there's no time to wait, and there's no choice)

I can't do that. It's dangerous.
I'll do that as soon as it's fixed.
I'm sorry but I'm not going to do it until it's fixed.

ROLE PLAY: Choose one situation above and act out what you would say if you decided to refuse to work.

STUDENT ACTION RESEARCH

OSHA FORMS: Get a complaint form from the OSHA office nearest you. In class, discuss the meaning of each part. Talk about a hazard that someone in class knows about. Tape record the story. With your teacher, write down the story and use the information from the story to fill out the form.

CODE WRITING: Develop a code about dangerous work. Make up discussion questions and talk about your answers. Figure out possible solutions and act out what you would do or say.

Lesson 4   After an Accident or Illness

CODE

Maria: What's the matter?

Mung: I hurt my back.

Maria: How did it happen?

Mung: I was helping a patient and she started to slip. I grabbed her and something snapped in my back.

Maria: You better tell your supervisor and go to the nurse.

Mung: I don't want to.

Maria: Why not?

Mung: He'll be mad. I've already missed too much work. And I don't want it on my record.

Maria: But if you're really hurt, you won't be able to collect.

Questions for discussion:

1. Where do Mung and Maria work?
  What's wrong with Mung?
  How did she get hurt?

2. What does Maria tell her to do? Why?
  What is Mung worried about? Why?

3. Have you ever had an accident at work? What happened?
  Did you report it? Why or why not?
  In your country, what happens if someone gets hurt at work? Do they
    get paid?

4. Do you think it's important to report accidents? Why or why not? What might happen if you do not report an accident?
5. What do you think Mung should do? Why?

ACTION ACTIVITIES

A. COMPETENCY: Reporting an accident

Every workplace has its own ways of reporting accidents. Usually, you tell your supervisor first. Then you may be sent to the nurse. Sometimes you fill out an accident report form. Find the lines in this conversation where the worker *gets the supervisor's attention, tells what happened,* and *tells how it happened.*

Worker: I'd like to report an accident.
Supervisor: What happened?
Worker: I was helping a patient and I hurt my back.
Supervisor: How did that happen?
Worker: I was walking her to the bathroom and she started to slip. I caught her, but something snapped in my back.
Supervisor: Is it bad?
Worker: I don't know, but it hurts.
Supervisor: You better fill out a form and get it checked.

Add to this list of ways to report an accident:

Getting Attention

I'd like to report an accident.
I want to report an accident.
I just got hurt.

Telling what happened/what is hurt

I bumped my head.
Make sentences for these injuries:
  (burned/leg)
  (twisted/ankle)
  (hurt/back)
  (got something in/eye)

Telling how or why it happened

A box fell on my foot. It was stored wrong.
I slipped in a puddle. There's a leak.

ROLE PLAY: Divide into pairs; each pair should act out reporting one of the following accidents:

1. A worker cut herself on some sharp parts.
2. A worker burned himself. Someone put a hot pan in the sink.
3. A worker hurt his neck. The brakes on the forklift didn't work and he hit a box.
4. A worker got something in her eye. She doesn't know what or how it happened.
5. A worker hurt his back. He slipped on some wet stairs.

B. COMPETENCY: Filling out accident and illness forms

Discuss each part of this form in class. In pairs, fill out the form for one of the accidents on the previous page. Share your work with other students.

EMPLOYEE ACCIDENT REPORT

DATE: ____/___/_____

NAME: _____ AGE: _____ SEX – F ☐
M ☐

DEPARTMENT: _____ JOB TITLE: _____

DEPT. SUPERVISOR: _____ IMMED. SUPERVISOR: _____

DETAILS OF ACCIDENT

DATE OF ACCIDENT: ____/___/_____

TIME: _____

(1) EXACT LOCATION: _____

_____

(2) EMPLOYEE'S DESCRIPTION OF INCIDENT:

_____

_____

_____

(3) WITNESS: _____
Signature

TIME LOST DUE TO ACCIDENT: _____

TREATMENT: _____

DEPARTMENT-HEAD COMMENTS – ACTION TAKEN:

_____

_____

_____
Signature

PRACTICE: One student should tell the class about an accident or illness at work. Tape record the story and write it down (your teacher may help you). Read the story together and ask the student questions about what happened. Look at the story and use the information to fill out an accident report form.

READING: Workers' compensation

Divide into groups; each group should read one question and report it to the others.

1. What are Workers' Compensation laws? Workers' Compensation laws in each state say that workers can get benefits for disabilities caused by work-related injuries or illnesses. A *disability* is a medical problem which stops you from doing your regular job. You cannot lose your job if you have a *temporary disability.*

2. What injuries and illnesses are covered? You can collect Workers' Compensation benefits (medical care and pay for lost wages):

—if you get hurt at work (and lose pay).

—if you get a disease (like lead poisoning or cancer) from work.

—if you have a medical problem which becomes disabling because of an injury at work.

—if you get hurt on company grounds (for example, the parking lot) on the way to or from work.

3. How do you collect Workers' Compensation? In order to collect, you should:

—Report your accident to your supervisor immediately. If you don't report it within three months, you may lose the right to collect.

—Report a job-related illness to your employer as soon as you know about it. If you don't report it within 120 days of knowing about it, you may lose the right to collect.

—Report to first aid or the nurse's office immediately. Tell how the injury happened.

—Do not sign any papers with empty blanks. Do not sign any papers that you do not understand. Show them to your union representative or another worker before signing them.

—Keep a copy of all accident report forms or other papers about the accident/ illness. Sometimes papers get lost. You may need to prove that you reported the accident on time.

—Keep the names and addresses of anyone who saw the accident (these people are *witnesses*).

—Keep all doctor's bills and statements about your injury.

—Make a *claim* for Workers' Compensation if you lose time from work. A claim is a request for payment. Often the claim form is the same as the *accident report form.* Your employer will send it in. *You should keep checking on it.*

COMPREHENSION

Do you think these workers can get Workers' Compensation? Write *yes* or *no* in the blank.

_____ **1.** Mario lost a finger on the job.

_____ **2.** Juan was in a car accident on the way to work. The accident was two miles from work.

_____ **3.** Mary had a history of back problems. She picked up something heavy at work and injured her back.

_____ **4.** A brick fell on Alda in the parking lot as she was leaving work.

_____ **5.** Jose hurt his back at work. He didn't report it. Four months later, an x-ray showed damage to his spine.

_____ **6.** Mel worked with heavy dust for several years. Ten years after he left the job, he got lung disease.

_____ **7.** Juanita hurt her foot at work; her boss gave her a job sitting down. She didn't miss any work.

STUDENT ACTION RESEARCH

1. Find out the procedures for reporting an accident at your workplace or a friend's workplace. You can ask these questions:

Who do you tell first?
What do you do if the injury is serious? Do you walk off the job and go to the nurse first? Or do you tell your supervisor first?
What do you do if you can't find the supervisor?
What will happen if you do not report an accident?
Where do you get accident report forms?
Bring an accident report form to class.

2. Can you collect Workers' Compensation if you are disabled because of stress? Who could help you find out the answer to this question? Find out the answer to these questions.

CODE WRITING: Have you ever tried to collect Workers' Compensation? What happened to you (how were you disabled)? What did you do to collect? Did you do all of the things listed in this book? How long did it take to get your money? Were there any problems getting your money? From your discussion, write a code and questions for discussion about collecting Workers' Compensation.

READING: Keeping your job after a disability

Read this passage. Discuss the italicized words.

If you cannot do your regular job anymore because you are *permanently* hurt or sick, will you lose your job? Maybe not. The Rehabilitation Act of 1973 protects workers with *handicaps*. Employers with *funding* from the *federal government* must make *reasonable* changes for disabled workers: they must change hours, *schedules*, jobs, or *facilities* so that you can keep working. If they don't, they can lose their federal funding.

> Example: Alphonse Joseph developed a heart problem. His doctors told him to work fewer hours, take more breaks and stop climbing ladders. When Joseph asked for these changes, his supervisor said no. Joseph's union said it would file a complaint. The company did not want to lose its government contracts so it made the changes.

To be covered by the Rehabilitation Act:

1. Your employer must have government contracts or funding.
2. Your handicap must be covered by the Act.
3. The changes made by the employer must not be too expensive or difficult.

In each of the following cases, do you think the person is covered by the Rehabilitation Act? What three questions would you ask to find out?

1. Maria has kidney problems. She wants to leave early for treatments.
2. Anna has leg braces. She wants to park in the supervisors' parking lot, close to the building.
3. Emma has arthritis. She wants a different job in her company.
4. George sprained his ankle. He wants a sitting job for a week.
5. Other (Add your own.) _____

STUDENT ACTION RESEARCH

1. Do you know anyone with a disability? Make a list of disabilities. Which ones are covered by the Rehabilitation Act? Try calling the Department of Health and Human Services in your city to find out. Put a check next to the disabilities covered by the Act.
2. Does an employer have federal contracts or funding? Think of one employer. Call the Office of Federal Contract Compliance Programs to find out if that employer does business with the federal government.

Lesson 5   Pregnancy on the Job

Maria: I just found out I'm pregnant.

Liz: That's great! How do you feel?

Maria: Good and terrible. I'm happy about being pregnant, but I don't feel well and I'm worried about working.

Liz: Why?

Maria: What if I can't do my job? What if I'm too sick or too tired? The company might not want to keep me.

Liz: You worry too much!

Maria: But I need the money. Will they pay me if I have to take a leave?

Liz: I'm not sure. Maybe you can ask for light duty.

Questions for discussion:

1. What did Maria find out?
    Is she sick?
    What is a *leave of absence*?
    What is *light duty*?

2. What is Maria worried about?
    What does she think might happen?
    How does she think the company will feel?

3. In your country, what happens when a working woman gets pregnant?
   Does she continue working? Does she get paid for leaves?
   Do you know any pregnant workers?
   How do other workers treat them? How does the employer treat them?
   Do they get light duty? How long do they work?
   Do they get paid leaves of absence?

4. What are some problems of pregnant workers?
   How do employers feel about pregnant workers? Why?

5. What do you think Maria should do?
   What do you think her employer should do?
   Do Liz and Maria know the rights of pregnant workers?
   What can pregnant workers do to protect their jobs?

THINKING ACTIVITIES

A. ATTITUDES ABOUT PREGNANCY AT WORK

Read these statements about pregnancy. First check *agree* or *disagree*.
Then discuss your answers in small groups.

	AGREE	DISAGREE
1. A pregnant worker should tell her boss as soon as she knows she is pregnant.	____	____
2. A woman should stop working when she knows she is pregnant.	____	____
3. The employer should pay for maternity leave.	____	____
4. If her job is too heavy, a pregnant woman should quit.	____	____
5. A woman should go back to work as soon as she can after her baby is born.	____	____
6. If a pregnant woman's job is unsafe, the employer should give her another job.	____	____
7. A pregnant woman should not get extra breaks. It's not fair to other workers.	____	____
8. An employer should let the woman work as long as she wants to.	____	____

B. GRAMMAR: Modals (may, might)

Add to these lists of the problems that a pregnant woman might have at work:

She might have morning sickness.
_____ be very tired.
_____ have back problems.
_____ swollen legs.
_____ (others)

Her legs might bother her.
Smells _____.
Her back _____.
Chemicals _____.
(others) _____.

C. VOCABULARY

Match these words with their meanings:

_____ **1.** leave of absence

_____ **2.** unpaid leave

_____ **3.** personal leave

_____ **4.** disability pay

_____ **5.** health insurance

_____ **6.** light duty

_____ **7.** maternity leave

a. pay for a long period when you cannot work because of an illness or injury (that you did not get at work)

b. period of time away from work with employers permission

c. money paid to doctor or hospital for medical care

d. easier job for worker who cannot do his or her regular job

e. period away from work with no disability pay or wages

f. period away from work because of pregnancy

g. period away from work for family or non-medical reasons

D. FINDING OUT YOUR RIGHTS (Grammar: if clauses)

There are some federal laws about pregnancy and work; other rights vary from state to state and job to job. Complete these questions and then read the legal information that follows to see which of these questions are covered by federal law. Who can answer the other questions?

1. (job/unsafe) If my job is unsafe, can my boss fire me?
2. (job/too heavy)
3. (I/sick)
4. (I/healthy)
5. (I/tired)

Make up other *if*-questions about pregnancy that begin like this:

Can I collect unemployment _____?

Can I take an unpaid leave _____?

Can I get a paid leave _____?

Add your own questions about pregnancy and work.

READING: Pregnancy rights

Divide into groups. Each group should read one story and report about it. Explain the legality of the story to the class.

1. HIRING: Bonnie Perez was offered a sales job at a store. She told the interviewer she was three months pregnant. He said that the store does not hire people who need early leaves of absence. He told her to apply again after the baby was born.

This was illegal: An employer cannot refuse to hire or promote a pregnant woman who can do the main functions of the job.

2. HEALTH INSURANCE: Soraya Martinez got pregnant. Her co-workers told her she would not be covered by health insurance because she was single.

They were wrong: Health insurance paid for by the employer must cover pregnancy if the worker is married or single. Health plans must also pay for the pregnancy of wives of male employees.

3. JOB SECURITY: Mei-Lin Lei worked in a nursing home. Her boss wanted her to take an unpaid leave in her fifth month of pregnancy. He said the work was too heavy. She felt fine and wanted to keep working. He told her to leave.

Her supervisor was wrong: You have the right to work if you can do your job. You can only be asked to go on leave if your doctor says you cannot do your job.

4. UNEMPLOYMENT BENEFITS: When Maria Monteiro got pregnant, the fumes at her job began to bother her. Her doctor wrote a note saying the job was dangerous. Maria wanted to work in another part of the plant while she was pregnant. Her boss said there were no openings. She asked for a leave of absence. Her boss laid her off and told her to collect unemployment.

Her supervisor was right: Pregnant women can collect unemployment if:

a. They cannot do their regular job.
b. Their doctor states in writing it is dangerous for the mother or baby.
c. They ask for a safer job but can't get it.
d. They ask for a leave of absence.
e. They are able and willing to do other work.

They cannot collect unemployment if they are unable to work. This means they cannot collect during a leave at the end of a pregnancy to give birth.

5. DISABILITY PAY AND BENEFITS: When Elsa Auerbach was six months pregnant, she had to take a leave of absence. Her back was bad and her doctor said she could not work. She had to stay out four months but the company only paid her for six weeks. It paid workers with other disabilities (heart attacks, broken bones, etc.) for the full time they were out.

In 1979, this became illegal. The law says that pregnancy must be treated like any other disability.

This means: The employer does *not* have to pay you during maternity leaves. But if the employer pays other disabled workers for leaves, pregnant women must also be paid.

CHECKING UP: Read these stories about pregnant workers. Answer the questions and explain your answers.

1. Emily applied for a better job in her company. She was healthy and able to do the job. Her employer told her to apply again after she had the baby. Was this legal?
2. Margo was not married when she got pregnant. Her doctor told her to go to a clinic because her insurance might not cover her. Was the doctor right?
3. Anna's doctor said her job was dangerous. She asked her boss for a lighter job. He told her to go on leave; usually workers at her job take a leave if they cannot do their regular job. There is no light duty. Could her supervisor make her go on leave?
4. Anna's supervisor (from story #3) told her to try to collect unemployment. Do you think she could collect?

ACTION ACTIVITIES

A. COMPETENCY: Requesting job changes

Act out this dialogue; find the lines where Maria *gets her supervisor's attention, states the problem,* and *requests a job change.*

Maria: Could I talk to you for a moment?

Supervisor: Sure. What's up?

Maria: I'm pregnant and these fumes are making me dizzy. I was wondering if you could transfer me to another job.

Supervisor: You better bring a note from your doctor.

Maria: OK. I will.

Add to these ways to *get attention, state the problem,* and *ask for a change.*

Getting Attention

Could I talk to you for a minute?
Do you have a minute?

Stating the Problem

I just found out I'm pregnant and . . .
    the fumes are bothering me.
    my back is bothering me.

Asking for a Change

I was wondering if I could work in another area.
Would it be possible to take a leave of absence?
I would like to go on light duty.
I need to go out on disability.
My doctor says I should stop working overtime.

ROLE PLAY: In pairs, act out requesting job changes using the following information.

Problem	Request
1. varicose veins	work sitting down
2. tired	stop working overtime
3. morning sickness	take a few weeks off
4. back problems	light duty
5. chemicals are dangerous	transfer to another job
6. (Add your own.)	

DISCUSSION: What can you do if your supervisor will not make changes? Whom can you ask for help at your workplace? Whom can you ask for help outside your workplace? What would happen if you insisted on your rights?

B. COMPETENCY: Insisting on rights

Act out the following dialogue. Find the lines where Maria *states her request* and *insists on her rights.*

Supervisor: I want you to go out on leave. You can't do this job. It's too heavy.

Maria: I feel fine. I'd like to keep working.

Supervisor: It might be dangerous. I don't want trouble.

Maria: My doctor says it's fine. You have to let me work if I can do the job.

Add to these ways to *state your request* and *state your rights*.

State your request

I would like light duty.
Could I get a job in another area?

State your rights

You have to treat me the same as other disabled workers.
You have to give me light duty if you give other workers light duty.

ROLE PLAY: In pairs, act out insisting on your rights for the following situations:

1. You want light duty.
2. You want a personal leave.
3. You want to keep working.
4. You want a different job.
5. You want extra relief time.
6. (Add your own.)

Remember: You do not have the right to these things if other workers at your job do not get them.

STUDENT ACTION RESEARCH

1. Interview a friend (or a co-worker) about pregnancy at their or your workplace. Add to this list of questions:

How long do pregnant workers usually work?
Do they ever get light duty?
Are they ever asked to quit or leave?
Do other disabled workers get disability pay or light duty? For how long?

2. If you are not working, interview someone who worked while she was pregnant. Add to this list of questions:

How did you feel? Did you have medical problems?
Did you have problems doing your job?
How did you solve the problems? Did you ask for light duty or another job?
    Did you go out on leave?

CODE WRITING: Make up a code about pregnancy at work.

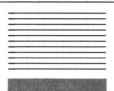

Moving Toward Equality

Lesson 1   Identifying Discrimination

CODE

Jean-Louis: I'm quitting.

Jose: How come?

Jean-Louis: I'm sick of washing dishes.

Jose: Are you going to look for another hotel job?

Jean-Louis: No way. I don't want to be stuck in the kitchen for the rest of my life.

Jose: Your English is good. Why don't you apply for a job at the front of the house?

Jean-Louis: Have you ever seen a Haitian working at the front desk?

Questions for discussion:

1. Where do Jean-Louis and Jose work?
   What does Jean-Louis do?
   What is the front of the house? The back of the house?
   Who works in the front of the house in this hotel? Who works in the back
      of the house?
2. Why is Jean-Louis quitting his job?
   What does Jose suggest?
   Why doesn't Jean-Louis think it's a good suggestion?
3. In your workplace, do immigrants and Americans have the same kinds
      of jobs?
   Do men and women have the same kinds of jobs?
   Do racial minorities and white people have the same kinds of jobs?
   In your country, are there different nationalities? Do they have an equal
      chance for all kinds of jobs?
4. What is *discrimination*?
   Why do you think some groups of people often get lower wages or
      worse jobs?
5. What do you think Jean-Louis should do?
   Have you ever felt that you were treated unfairly because you are an
      immigrant? What happened? What did you do? What could you do?

THINKING ACTIVITIES

A. VOCABULARY

Discuss the meanings of these words. Then make sentences from your own
experience that show the meanings.

1. discrimination, discriminate against: In my country, some employers
   discriminate against women. Women cannot get jobs as supervisors.
2. equality, equal:
3. race, racial:
4. nationality:
5. sex:
6. age:
7. ethnic group:
8. religion/religious:
9. handicap:
10. minority:

Read each of these stories. Write the words that describe the kind of
discrimination after the story.

1. Joe works for a computer company. He is fifty years old. Joe applied for
   a special training program but only younger workers with less qualifications were accepted. *age discrimination*
2. Maria is a waitress. She wants a bartender's job. She has experience,
   but her boss wants only men at the bar.
3. A man and a woman got in a fight at work. The woman was suspended
   but the man was fired.
4. Mung works as a light housekeeper. She does the same thing as Thang,
   but he is in heavy housekeeping. He gets paid more.

5. Chi-Wei applied for a promotion. He was more experienced than an American, but the American got the job. The job did not require much English, but his supervisor said his English wasn't good enough.

6. John was fired for refusing to work on Saturdays. He is black. Several white workers refused to work Saturdays and did not get fired.

B. READING: Ray Lee's story

Ray Lee, who has a masters degree in electrical engineering, has worked as a subway repairman since 1977. He has never been absent and hasn't made any mistakes on this job. He applied for a promotion last year. He was interviewed but never got an answer; the job was given to a less qualified non-minority person. Lee said:

> I can't get the job maybe because I can't speak fluent English. Anyway, the guy who got it is supervising me—I may get in trouble if I go to protest. I have to stay in my job and wait for another chance. . . . By the way, it is very difficult to prove that the authorities discriminate against you.

Questions for discussion:

1. Where does Ray Lee work?
2. How much education does he have?
3. What did he do last year?
4. Who got the job?
5. Why does Ray Lee think he didn't get the job?
6. What is he going to do about it?
7. Why is he not going to protest?
8. What do you think Ray Lee should do? First answer individually, then try to decide on a group answer.

READING: Discrimination laws

Divide into groups. Each group should read one question and report on it to the class.

1. What kinds of discrimination are illegal? Title VII of the Civil Rights Act of 1964 is the most important federal law against job discrimination. It says that employment decisions cannot be based on *race, color, national origin, sex, age,* or *religion.* You have the right to be judged on your ability, qualifications, and experience as an individual. States also have their own laws against discrimination. For example, in some states it is illegal to discriminate against handicapped people.

2. Who does Title VII cover? Anyone who works for an employer with fifteen or more employees.

3. What does Title VII say? Employers cannot discriminate in *hiring, promotions, discharge, pay, benefits,* or other aspects of employment on the basis of race, color, national origin, sex, age, or religion. For example, an employer cannot refuse to hire you or promote you because you belong to a minority group. An employer cannot fire you or give less pay or fewer benefits because you belong to a minority group.

4. What does Title VII NOT say? Title VII does not say that decisions based on looks, friendships, family ties, or marital status are illegal. This means an employer can favor friends, relatives, or people who are single.

5. How can you prove discrimination? To prove discrimination, you need to show that:

You are a member of a protected group (woman, black, ethnic minority, etc.).

You were treated unfairly because you are a member of this group (not for some other reason like family favoritism).

You are equally qualified or experienced as the person chosen.

Any differences (in experience, language, etc.) are not important for the job.

It also helps to show that others in your group have been treated unfairly.

6. What are some regulations against discrimination in hiring?

A woman cannot be rejected for a job because she doesn't look strong enough or because she is pregnant.

The employer cannot demand more experience or education than necessary for a job if the reason or effect is to exclude minorities.

A person cannot be rejected for a job because of poor English unless good English is necessary for the job.

COMPREHENSION: Do you think the people in these stories are protected by Title VII?

1. A woman is a dishwasher in a restaurant. Eight people work there. The men dishwashers are paid more than the women.
2. Ten Haitians work in a shoe factory. Five of them work in better-paying jobs. Five work in the lowest-paying jobs. One applies for a promotion but doesn't get it. The employer says he doesn't have enough experience. An American worker with more experience gets the promotion.
3. There are 50 black workers and 20 white workers in one department. They have similar qualifications and experience. The company opens a training program. Six white workers and two black workers are accepted into it.
4. There are four job openings at a large restaurant. You tell your friends to apply. The supervisor's four sons also apply. The four sons get the jobs.
5. A woman works in an office as a clerk. She has the same job as a male co-worker. He gets benefits but she doesn't. Her boss says she doesn't need them because she's married.
6. A woman applies for a job lifting heavy pipes. She had worked as a truck driver before, loading and unloading steel. She does not get the job: the interviewer didn't think she looked strong enough. She wasn't given a strength test or a chance to do the job. A man is hired.
7. A Filipino-American dental worker at a university dental school was refused a supervisory job because the university said his accent was too strong. His English was good enough to communicate and do a supervisor's job.
8. (Add your own.)

MATCHING: The law says that there can be no discrimination in promotions, job evaluations, work rules, and work assignments. Match each of these statements with one of the stories below.

_____ **1.** It is illegal to promote men with fewer qualifications ahead of more qualified women.

_____ **2.** When an employer promotes white employees ahead of minorities, he or she must have good reasons for the choice.

_____ **3.** Job evaluations by supervisors must be objective and not open to the personal bias of supervisors.

_____ **4.** Men and women must have the same work rules, vacations, rest periods, and freedom to talk on the job.

_____ **5.** Employees may not be separated by race or nationality.

_____ **6.** Workers cannot be required to speak only English unless it is necessary for the job.

a. The owner of a plastics factory makes everyone at work speak English even though many workers are Vietnamese and don't know the language very well.

b. Only black park workers are assigned to a mainly black neighborhood of the city.

c. A class-action suit showed that a telephone company systematically denied promotions to women and minorities; only white men were promoted to top management jobs. Most of the employees were women but only 1 percent of management were women. The company had to pay $15 million in back pay and $38 million in wage adjustments. Several thousand women and minorities were promoted.

d. At an auto plant, hourly workers needed recommendations from their foremen to get promotions. Few blacks received them. The black employees went to court and won. The court said that the procedure for recommendations depended too much on the foreman's personal opinion.

e. At an electronics plant, only men were allowed to smoke while working. Men were allowed to line up at the clocks before quitting time, but women had to keep working.

READING: Voices from History

Raymond Dubois worked for the Amoskeag Manufacturing Company, once the world's largest textile factory. Here he talks about the factory fifty years ago.

Dubois: I think immigrants were kept down, because if there was a choice to promote somebody, it wouldn't be the immigrant. You'd have to be exceptional. They'd have to need them for a job that nobody else would touch. If, for instance, an individual was an exceptional man with his hands . . . he might receive better pay but only if they didn't have anybody else that could do it better. If a boss was Irish, he took care of the Irish; if he was French, he'd take care of the French. At that time, the French and the Irish were the stronger faction here in the city, and the Greeks and Polish did the work.

ACTION ACTIVITIES

A. COMPETENCY: Identifying discrimination

Make lists of "good" and "not good" jobs at your workplace. If you do not work, choose jobs from a public place (a hospital, a school, or store).

Good jobs	Your list	Not good jobs	Your list
manager	_____	dishwasher	_____
doorman	_____	housekeeper	_____
front desk	_____		_____

MAP/CHART: Now make a map of the workplace which shows where different jobs are located. Write *I* for immigrants on the map; write *W* for women; write *M* for minorities. Or make a chart like this one for your workplace:

Good jobs	Women	Minorities	Immigrants
manager	0	0	0
doorman	0	2	1
front desk	4	2	0
Not good jobs			
housekeeper	all	many	many
dishwasher	0	many	many

What patterns do you see on your charts or maps? Who has the best jobs? Who has the worst jobs? Why?

B. COMPETENCY: Requesting a promotion

CHART: Make a chart with the advantages and disadvantages of promotions. Why might someone want a promotion? Why might they *not* want a promotion?

DIALOGUE: Look at the conversation on page 126. In which line does Jean-Louis do each of the following:

—explain that he wants a promotion?
—discuss his language abilities?
—describe his present work situation?
—discuss his interest/reason for wanting the change?
—discuss his qualifications?
—show that he's aware of possible discrimination?
—ask about job training?
—show that he will not drop his request?

Jean-Louis: I'd like to talk to you about promotions. I want to apply for the job at the front desk.

Personnel: Where do you work now?

Jean-Louis: In the kitchen. I wash dishes.

Personnel: People don't usually switch departments. Why don't you look for something else in the kitchen?

Jean-Louis: I'd like to get out of the kitchen. I'd like to work with the customers.

Personnel: Your English needs to be very good and you need special training to work at the front desk.

Jean-Louis: I've studied English for five years. My supervisor says it's excellent. I also speak three other languages so I could help foreign guests. Could you tell me about the training?

Personnel: It takes a long time. We only offer it twice a year.

Jean-Louis: How do I apply for it?

Personnel: First, I better talk to your supervisor.

Jean-Louis: I'm very interested in the job. I think it would be good for the hotel to have minorities at the front desk.

Personnel: Fill out this form and I'll get back to you.

Jean-Louis: Thank you. I'll check back in a week if I haven't heard from you.

Make a list of possible answers for these questions:

1. Can I help you?
2. What do you do now?
3. What job do you want?
4. Why do you want to change jobs?
5. Do you think you can do this job?
6. I'm not sure your English is good enough.

ROLE PLAY: Think of a job you would like and could do at your workplace. Act out what you would say to ask for a promotion.

C. COMPETENCY: Acting for equality at work

Add to this list of things you can do if you think you are being discriminated against:

1. *Work with a group of co-workers:* Often if a group of workers talks to the employer about unequal treatment, there will be a change; the employer does not want to be charged with discrimination.
2. *File a grievance:* If you're in a union, your union representative may help you correct the problem.
3. *File a complaint with a government agency:* You can file a complaint with the Equal Employment Opportunity Commission (EEOC) or with a state commission.
4. *File a lawsuit:* You can also file a lawsuit if you first file a complaint with a government agency.

ROLE PLAY: Look at Ray Lee's story on page 122. Divide into groups. Each group should act out a different way Ray Lee could take action about his problem. Here are some suggestions. Add your own.

1. Ray Lee is talking to another worker. The other worker suggests filing a discrimination grievance with the union. Ray doesn't want to do anything.
2. Ray decides to talk to his supervisor about the problem and ask for a chance at the next job opening.
3. Ray calls the EEOC to get information about how to file a discrimination charge.
4. Ray reports the problem to the EEOC. He tells what happened and why he thinks it is discrimination.

ROLE PLAY: Use a real story from a class member. First show what happens to the student and then act out three separate possible ways of handling the problem. Discuss what was good and bad about each solution.

STUDENT ACTION RESEARCH

Find out the name and phone number of the state commission against discrimination in your state. Find out the phone number of the EEOC in your city. Get a copy of the complaint forms and read them in class. Fill them out for one example of discrimination from your experience.

ORAL HISTORY: Interview one person about his or her experience as a minority worker. Tape the story and write it.

Lesson 2   Men's Work, Women's Work

CODE

Mari: I think I'm going to apply for that job in transportation. I want to get out of housekeeping.

Alicia: You can't do that. You have to be strong to lift the patients and push their wheelchairs or stretchers.

Mari: Well, I lift all kinds of things now. I move beds and carry supplies. I know I'm strong enough.

Alicia: But transportation is a man's job. Why do you want to do that?

Mari: I want to move around more. And the pay is better.

Alicia: Really? Their work isn't any harder than ours. It doesn't take more skill. Maybe I should apply, too!

Questions for discussion:

1. What job does Mari have now? What does she do?
  What job does Mari want? What would she do?

2. Which job is harder, housekeeping or transportation?
  Who works in transportation now?
  Why does Mari want to work in transportation?
  Is Mari strong enough for a transportation job?

3. In your country, do women often work outside the home?
Are there men's jobs and women's jobs? What are they?
In your workplace, are there men's jobs and women's jobs?
Do you know a woman who has done a "man's job"?
Do you know a man who has done a "woman's job"?

4. What kinds of jobs are usually filled by women? Why?
What kinds of jobs are usually filled by men? Why?
Why do you think more and more women are working?
Why do you think women's jobs are usually paid less? Why is this
changing?

5. Do you think Mari should apply for the new job?
What can women do to get equal pay with men?
What can women do to get into "men's jobs"?

THINKING ACTIVITIES

A. EXPRESSING OPINIONS ABOUT WOMEN AT WORK

Check *agree* or *disagree* for each sentence. Discuss your answers in small
groups. Present your opinions to the class with reasons. Use phrases like
these to express opinions:

> I feel that women should work at any job they want to.
> In my opinion, women should not do heavy jobs.
> We don't think that women should work while their children are small.

Note: Do not use both *in my opinion* and *I think that* in the same sentence.

	AGREE	DISAGREE
1. Jobs are not as important for women. Men should get the better jobs because they have to support their families.	——	——
2. Women should not do heavy or dangerous jobs. They aren't strong enough and might hurt themselves.	——	——
3. A women should have the chance to do any job she wants to do.	——	——
4. Women are better at some kinds of jobs (teacher, nurse, secretary) so they should get these jobs.	——	——
5. If a man and a woman are equally qualified for a good job, the woman should get it because there are fewer women in good jobs.	——	——
6. Women should not work when their children are small. They should stay home until their children are in school.	——	——
7. If women fight for equality, men will be hurt. Men's pay will be lower and they will get worse jobs.	——	——

B. READING: Mung and Em's story

Mung and Em were married for five years in Vietnam before they came to the United States. Em was a mechanic and Mung stayed home with their daughter. They have been in the U.S. for three years. They have another child. Em works in a factory, but doesn't earn much.

Mung wants to work. She wants to help with the bills and to get out of the house. Em is worried that their family life will change if she works. He thinks she should stay home with the children. He thinks she may become too independent and may not listen to him anymore. He thinks she will be too tired to take care of the house. But he is also worried about paying the bills. What should they do?

Personal Opinion   Group Opinion

_____   _____

_____   _____

Do you know anyone else with the same problem? What did they do? What happened? Tell their story and write it in the Log.

C. COMPARING WAGES (Grammar: comparative phrases)

Even though discrimination is illegal, there are still many inequalities: men and women often get different kinds of jobs. Women's wages are often lower, especially for minority women. From the information on the chart, complete the sentences. Note the use of comparison words: *most, least, highest, lowest, more than, less than, higher than, lower than, the same as, as much as, equal to.*

MEDIAN INCOMES OF FULL-TIME WORKERS IN ALL
OCCUPATIONS (1981)

White Men	$21,178	White Women	$12,665
Black Men	$14,984	Black Women	$11,438
Hispanic Men	$14,981	Hispanic Women	$11,917

1. White men earned the most. They earned almost twice as much
   as _____.
2. Black men earned less than white men. They earned about as much
   as _____.
3. Black women earned the least. They earned almost as much as
   _____.
4. White women's wages were less than any men's wages. They were more
   than _____.
5. Hispanic men's wages were lower than other men's. They were higher
   than _____.
6. Black men's wages were about the same as Hispanic men's wages. Both
   were less than _____.
7. Hispanic women's wages were almost equal to _____.

Now look at the following chart and make up sentences using these comparison words:

1. more than _____

2. equal to _____

3. almost as much as _____

4. the least _____

5. the lowest _____

6. higher than _____

7. the same as _____

8. almost half as much as _____

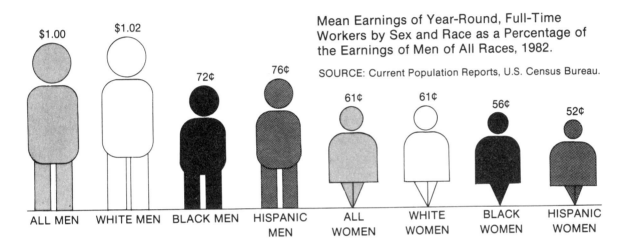

Mean Earnings of Year-Round, Full-Time Workers by Sex and Race as a Percentage of the Earnings of Men of All Races, 1982.

SOURCE: Current Population Reports, U.S. Census Bureau.

D. DISCUSSION

Why do you think there are such big differences in wages among different groups?

READING: Legal Information on equal pay

Divide into groups. Each group should read one question and report on it to the class:

What does the Equal Pay Act of 1963 say? This Act says that men and women must be paid equal wages for equal work in the same workplace. It is illegal to pay men and women different wages for the same or similar work.

> Example: The Miller Brewing Company paid women technicians in one laboratory 70 cents per hour less than men technicians doing the same work in another laboratory. The women brought suit under the Equal Pay Act and won: their pay was raised and they got several years' lost wages.

The law says: There can be pay differences for reasons other than sex (for example, seniority). This means if women were not hired until recently, their wages may be lower because they have less seniority.

The law says: Men are also protected: their wages cannot be lowered to equal women's wages. The lower wages will be raised. Men can file complaints if they are paid less than women doing the same work.

How do you file a complaint? You can phone or file a written complaint with the Equal Employment Opportunity Commission (EEOC). You can also file a lawsuit. Equal pay complaints are confidential. The employer is not told who filed the complaint. It is illegal to retaliate against people who complain.

What jobs are "equal"? To be called equal, men's and women's jobs must require the same *skill*, *effort*, and *responsibility*. *Working conditions* must be similar. They do not have to be in the same department or have the same name.

Skill: People who have more training, education and experience and who use it on the job may be paid more.

Effort: People who do harder physical or mental work may be paid more.

Responsibility: People who supervise others or who make important decisions may be paid more.

Working Conditions: People who work in more dangerous conditons may be paid more.

ACTION ACTIVITIES

In small groups, read the story and answer the questions.

There are nine employees in the light housekeeping department at City Hospital, six women and three men. They are paid 50 cents per hour less than the men in heavy housekeeping, but their work is the same.

What should they do? First, list all their choices and then choose the best solution.

DISCUSSION: Present your group solution to the class. Can these workers ask for equal pay under the Equal Pay Act? Whom can you ask for more information? Find out the answer to the question.

ROLE PLAY: Act out three possible ways that the workers could handle this problem. Whom would they speak to? What would they say? What would be the consequences of their action?

STUDENT ACTION RESEARCH

1. Think of two jobs, one that is usually a woman's job and one that is usually a man's job. Answer these questions:

　a. How much skill is used on each job? Is more training, education, or experience necessary for either job?

　b. How much effort is required for each job? Do they require the same amount of physical or mental work most of the time?

　c. How much responsibility does each job have? Does either person make more decisions or supervise others?

　d. Are the working conditions similar for each job? Is one job more dangerous?

　e. What is the pay for each job?

　Is there a problem here? If so, what could be done about it?

2. There is presently a controversy about *comparable worth*. What is comparable worth? What is the controversy about? Invite a speaker to class to talk about it.

READING: Twice as Good a Job

by Hoagie Seibert, painting contractor

I GREW UP A TOMBOY,
SO I ALWAYS USED TOOLS,
AND I ALWAYS DID THINGS
THAT WERE PHYSICALLY HARD.
SO, TO ME,
IT WAS NATURAL
TO DO THIS KIND
OF WORK.

SOME WOMEN GROW UP
WORKING.
AND I FIND THAT THOSE WOMEN
MAKE GOOD PAINTERS.

IT'S TRUE
THAT YOU HAVE TO DO
TWICE AS GOOD A JOB
WHEN YOU'RE A WOMAN . . .

FOR INSTANCE,
I HURT MY BACK
RECENTLY.
I WASN'T SUPPOSED
TO LIFT ANYTHING.
WHEN I GOT
TWO FIVE-GALLON CANS
OF PAINT
AT THE PAINT STORE,
I REALLY WANTED
TO ASK FOR HELP
CARRYING IT,
BUT I DIDN'T.
I FELT FUNNY
ASKING MY HELPERS
TO LIFT FOR ME.
IF I WASN'T A WOMAN,
I WOULDN'T HAVE THOUGHT
ANYTHING OF IT.
BUT, AS A WOMAN,
I FEEL THAT
I HAVE TO PROVE MYSELF.

Questions for discussion:

1. Is Hoagie a man or a woman? How do you know?
2. What work does she do?
3. Is this usually a man's or a woman's job?
4. Why does she say some women make good painters?
5. What does the title of this poem mean?
6. What happened in the paint store?
7. Why didn't Hoagie ask for help?
8. Have you ever done a job that usually is done by the other sex? How did you feel?
9. What does Hoagie mean when she says "As a woman, I feel that I have to prove myself"?
10. Do you ever feel that you have to prove yourself?

Lesson 3   The Double Shift: After Work

CODE

Maria: You look tired.

Jan: I am. I was up till midnight again.

Maria: How come?

Jan: I had a lot to do after work. The kids didn't get to bed till nine. Then I had to clean up, do the wash, and do some cooking.

Maria: What was your husband doing?

Jan: After dinner he watched T.V. for a while and then he had to do his homework for English class.

Maria: Did you get your homework done?

Jan: Are you kidding?

Questions for discussion:

1. Does Jan work? Does her husband work?
   What did Jan do after work?
   What did her husband do after work?
2. Why is Jan tired?
   When does Jan relax? When does her husband relax?
   Does her husband have time to study English? Why or why not?
   Does Jan have time to study English? Why or why not?
   How many jobs does Jan have? What are they?

3. What do you do after work?
   When do you relax? When do you study English?
   Who usually does the housework in your country?
   Has this changed for you in the U.S.? Why?
4. Do you think housework is "real" work?
   Are some jobs around the house "women's jobs"? Why?
   Are some jobs around the house "men's jobs"? Why?
5. Should a husband and wife both study English?
   If two people in a family work, who do you think should do the housework?
   What can you do to share housework?

THINKING ACTIVITIES

A. INTERVIEWS: Your country vs. the U.S.

Interview each other about family work in your country and in the U.S. Make *who* questions about the jobs on the chart.

> Example: Who does the dishes in your country?

IN YOUR COUNTRY	wife	husband	children	grandparent
a. do laundry	——	——	——	——
b. take care of children	——	——	——	——
c. punish children	——	——	——	——
d. do dishes	——	——	——	——
e. fix car	——	——	——	——
f. mop floor	——	——	——	——
g. cook	——	——	——	——
h. earn money	——	——	——	——
I. shop for food	——	——	——	——
J. fix things in house	——	——	——	——

IN YOUR HOME IN THE U.S.	wife	husband	children	grandparent
a. do laundry	___	___	___	___
b. take care of children	___	___	___	___
c. punish children	___	___	___	___
d. do dishes	___	___	___	___
e. fix car	___	___	___	___
f. mop floor	___	___	___	___
g. cook	___	___	___	___
h. earn money	___	___	___	___
I. shop for food	___	___	___	___
J. fix things in house	___	___	___	___

DISCUSSION: Which things have changed? Why have they changed? How do you feel about the changes? Have they caused any problems? How can you solve them?

B. COLLAGES

Collect ads from magazines with pictures of women in them.

1. Practice reading the words in the ads.
2. Talk about the women in the ads.
   Who are they? What do you think they do?
   What do they look like?
   How old are they?
   What are they doing?
   How are their lives like yours?
   How are their lives different?
3. Make a list like this of all the people *you* are:

WHO ARE YOU?
student   _____
cook   _____
_____   _____
_____   _____
_____   _____

4. Draw pictures or bring in photos of your family life at home. Talk about what you and people in your family are doing in the pictures. Make a story with your pictures. Write about what is happening in your pictures.

C. BALANCING HOME AND WORK DEMANDS

Do you ever stay out of work because of family problems? Which do you think is more important, taking care of family problems or working? Read these stories. For each story, think of several solutions. Present them to the group. List all the possible solutions on the board. Choose the one you think is best and then find a group solution.

1. Maria has been at her job for six months. Her son is very sick: the doctor wants Maria to bring him in for tests. Maria has already missed work four times. She is worried about missing work.

   Personal solution: _____

   Group solution: _____

2. Chandara has been at his job a few months. He has been out sick four times. His father wants help buying a car and asks Chandara to stay out of work and come to the dealer with him. What should Chandara do?

   Personal solution: _____

   Group solution: _____

READING: Interview with Chha Vy

by Shirley Mark Yuen

Chha Vy is a twenty-nine year old Cambodian woman who has lived in Boston since October 1983. She is married and has a 1½ year old son and a 3 year old daughter.

SMY: When did you leave Cambodia and where did you go?

Chha Vy: I left my home (Phnom Penh, capital of Cambodia) in March 1982. I went with my husband to Battam Bang, a city near Thailand, because he knew it would be easier to escape there. In June of that year, we escaped to Khao I Dang camp in Thailand.

SMY: What was it like in refugee camp?

Chha Vy: It's hard to say. In some ways it was more difficult than in my home country. The U.S. government had control over everything. They distributed food, but there was never enough. Some refugees grew food in front of their houses and sold it to other refugees. Also, I was pregnant with my daughter at the time. The doctors were good, but I was always hungry. I never had enough food. The pregnant women in the camp were more lucky than others because sometimes we got fruit. They would give us powdered milk, cheese, and sometimes a little fruit (half a banana or a small orange), or a small biscuit. The American government didn't know Cambodian people didn't like milk and cheese. We would go for the fruit but throw away the milk and cheese. We didn't want to throw away food, but otherwise we couldn't get fruit. When my daughter was born, she was only five pounds.

SMY: How did you find Boston when you first arrived?

Chha Vy: There were so many changes; it was hard. It was winter and cold; I couldn't get used to the cold weather. I missed my family and worried about them. I was very lonely. My husband went to study English, but I couldn't since I was pregnant. I never wanted to leave the house. Our apartment was cold and dark, and I had no friends.

SMY: What is your relationship with your husband?

Chha Vy: Things are very different now—not like in Cambodia. When we first got married, we did everything together. We owned a small jewelry store so we worked together. We did many things together—visit friends and do fun things. Now, since we have been here, we are too busy to spend time together. Both of us study English, so we take turns taking care of the children. When I return from school, he goes. We never go out. This has been hard for both of us.

SMY: Have there been changes in your relationship?

Chha Vy: Oh, yes. In Cambodia, men never take care of children. My husband never expected to take care of children. Now we must help each other. Sometimes he will help me with the housework. In my country, women stayed at home and did the housework. Now, in America, they must go to work and still do the housework—and take care of the children. I can never tell my husband what to do. If he wants to help me, it is up to him. I think this is true for all Cambodian women. My husband is pretty good—better than some other men.

SMY: Who takes care of the household issues?

Chha Vy: Usually the husband. He takes care of all business, but I take care of the finances. For example, if someone was needed to visit the day care center, or there were problems with the landlord, my husband would be the one to go. But I keep the money. I think Cambodian women usually keep the money because men like to spend money—go out to restaurants to eat, and buy things. If the women are responsible, more money will be saved. It's better for the family. The women are always smart. They may hide the money for emergencies, but not ever let their husbands know they have it.

SMY: What do you want for your children?

Chha Vy: I want them to have a better life than I did—better than (the war) in my home country. I want them to have opportunities to study, to get good jobs, to have freedom, and to become good people. I want them to to be both American and and Cambodian. For example, I want them to learn to live like Americans, but I want them to keep their Cambodian culture. I heard from many people that Americans aren't nice to their parents. After they get married and move away, they don't visit or think about their parents very much. I think about my parents all the time. I care about my parents and I want my children to do the same for me.

SMY: What do you want for your future?

Chha Vy: I don't want to be evicted again. I've been evicted twice already—once for having too many people in one apartment, and once because the landlord raised our rent and we didn't have enough money to pay. I also don't want to continue getting welfare. I feel embarrassed about using food stamps. When I go to American markets (like Stop & Shop), I don't want to use food stamps because the American people give me dirty looks. It's better in Chinatown.

SMY: Do you think things will change later?

Chha Vy: I hope so. Now it is very hard. I go to school in the morning and my husband goes in the afternoon, so we never see each other. I want us both to get good jobs so we can do things on the weekends and have more for our children. Then we won't have to worry about so many things.

ACTION ACTIVITIES

A. COMPETENCY: Giving advice

Act out the conversation between Jill and Mie, adding Mie's advice to Jill. Use expressions like these to give advice:

> Maybe you should tell your supervisor the problem.
> Couldn't you ask a neighbor to look in on her.
> If I were you, I would stay home.

Mie: You look worried.

Jill: My daughter's sick.

Mie: What's wrong?

Jill: I don't know. She has a fever.

Mie: Who's taking care of her?

Jill: She's home by herself.

Mie: Do you think that's safe?

Jill: No, but I can't take any more time out. I already missed three days this month when my son had the flu. What can I do?

Mie: _____

ROLE PLAY: Act out these problems; one student tells about his/her problem and the other gives advice.

1. Your son is having trouble in school. His teacher wants you to come in for a conference at 3:30. You don't get out of work until 4:00. It takes an hour to get to the school by bus. Your supervisor wants you to work overtime.
2. Your daughter has a toothache. The dentist can only see her at 10:00 a.m. tomorrow (during your working hours). The next time he could see her is in ten days.
3. Your brother is arriving from Thailand. You are his only family in the U.S. His plane gets in during your working hours. You are still on probation at a new job.
4. A close friend of the family died. The funeral is during your working hours. The family would be very upset if you did not go to the funeral. You have already missed too much work.
5. (Add your own.)

B. COMPETENCY: Requesting time off

Copy these lines on another piece of paper and cut them apart. Divide into pairs; one person takes John's lines and the other takes the supervisor's lines. Put the sentences together in a conversation that makes sense.

John: I'd like to take the day off to get ready.

John: Could I talk to you for a minute?

John: The plane gets in Monday, the ninth at 2:30.

John: OK. Thanks a lot.

John: My brother is arriving from Thailand next week and I would like to meet him at the airport.

Supervisor: When do you want to leave?

Supervisor: Monday is a busy day. Why don't you leave at noon?

Supervisor: Sure. What's up?

Supervisor: When is he coming?

Find the lines in the conversation where John *gets the supervisor's attention, makes the request* (with the date he would like off), and *states the reason*.

Add to these lists of phrases to use in requesting time off:

Get attention

I'd like to ask you something.
I have a favor to ask.

Make the request

I was wondering if I could have next Tuesday off.
I'd like to leave early on Friday, May 13.

State the reason

My parents are arriving from Portugal.

Discuss what each of these supervisors' *responses* means:

I'll have to think about it.   I'll get back to you.
I'll let you know.   I think that's fine.
Sorry, but we're too busy.   Sorry, but too many people are out.
You've already missed too much.

Add to these ways of *persuading* your supervisor:

How about if I come in at noon? I'll make the time up.
It's the only appointment I can get.

DISCUSSION: When should you ask for time off? Make a list of things
to think about in timing your request (like your supervisor's mood, how
busy it is).

ROLE PLAY: Act out requesting time off for the situations on page 139.

STUDENT ACTION RESEARCH

INTERVIEWS: Interview three friends or co-workers about family problems
that interfered with work. Ask them what happened, what they did, and
how they solved their problems. Report back to class.

LOG: Write your own story: How do you balance your work, family, and
own needs? What problems are there? What can you do to solve them?
Add some stories to the class log.

Lesson 4   Sexual Harassment

CODE

Maria: Johnny is driving me crazy. Every time I walk by, he whistles and says something to the other men. Then they all laugh. It makes me feel cheap.

Alice: Don't worry. You'll get used to it. He does that to all of us. It's no big deal.

Maria: But it makes me nervous. I don't want to get used to it. I want to work somewhere else, not near him.

Alice: No wonder he whistles at you. You wear such nice clothes. Maybe you shouldn't dress so well.

Maria: But I like to look good.

Alice: Well, you just have to put up with men's comments then. If you don't like it, don't work with men.

Maria: But I need this job.

Alice: Then don't complain.

Questions for discussion:

1. What does Johnny do when Maria walks by?
Does he do the same thing to other women?
How does Maria look?

2. How does Maria feel? Why?
How does Alice feel? Why?
What does Alice think Maria should do? Why?
How does Maria feel about Alice's advice?

3. Do you know anyone who has had problems with the opposite sex at work? What happened? What did they do?

In your country, is it OK for men to whistle at women at work? Is it OK to touch women or ask them out?

4. Why do men whistle or make comments about women at work? Do you think that this kind of behavior is OK? What kinds of sexual behavior are problems at work? Why?

5. What do you think Maria should do? Do women have to put up with this kind of behavior at work? What can workers do about unwanted sexual behavior?

THINKING ACTIVITIES

A. IDENTIFYING SEXUAL HARASSMENT

COMPARING CULTURES: Here are some complaints about sexual harassment from women workers.* In your culture, which behaviors are common and acceptable at work? Which ones make you feel uncomfortable? First answer the questions for your culture and then answer the questions for yourself. Check "?" for behaviors that you aren't sure about or that are sometimes OK (depending on the situation).

	For my culture			For myself		
	OK	Not OK	?	OK	Not OK	?
1. A co-worker always whistles at me.	—	—	—	—	—	—
2. The men often make sexual comments about me.	—	—	—	—	—	—
3. The men call us sexual names.	—	—	—	—	—	—
4. A co-worker makes sexual jokes around me.	—	—	—	—	—	—
5. My boss is always touching and pinching me.	—	—	—	—	—	—
6. My boss keeps asking me out.	—	—	—	—	—	—
7. A co-worker keeps asking for sexual favors.	—	—	—	—	—	—
8. My boss said I'll get a raise if I sleep with him.	—	—	—	—	—	—

DISCUSSION: If you checked "?," explain when and why this behavior is OK in your culture. For each situation, explain what you would say or do in your culture.

RANKING: Rank the kinds of harassment from least to most serious. Discuss your answers.

---

*Male workers are also sometimes subject to harassment. However, this chapter mainly discusses harassment of women workers because this is a more common problem.

B. ATTITUDES TOWARD SEXUAL HARASSMENT

Here are some common attitudes about sexual harassment. Check *agree* or *disagree* for each of them. Discuss your answers. What would you say to someone with these views?

	AGREE	DISAGREE
1. Most women who are harassed ask for it by the way they dress, walk, or act. It's their own fault; they deserve what they get.	——	——
2. Sexual jokes are childish and rude.	——	——
3. There are more important things to worry about than sexual harassment.	——	——
4. Sexual comments are part of men's nature. You just have to accept it.	——	——
5. Men who harass women are insecure.	——	——

C. CULTURAL CONFLICT

An Indian hospital worker asked a co-worker to go out with him. When she refused, he kept asking. She tried to ignore him until he said he wanted to go home with her. When she told him to leave her alone, he got angry. She was afraid he might hurt her, so she told her boss. When the boss gave him a warning, the man was completely surprised. He thought his behavior was normal and couldn't understand why there was a problem. He said, "If she didn't want to be asked out, she shouldn't dress that way," and "When a woman refuses, you have to try harder."

1. What did the Indian man do?
2. What did the woman do?
3. How did the woman feel?
4. How did the man feel? Why do you think he acted this way?
5. Do you think the woman did the right thing?
6. What do you think the boss should do?
7. Do you think this is sexual harassment or cultural misunderstanding or both?
8. How should you act if the social rules for your culture are different from rules in the U.S.?

READING: Legal information about sexual harassment

Divide into groups. Each group should read one question and report on it to the class.

1. What is sexual harassment? According to the Equal Employment Opportunities Commission (EEOC), it is any sexual attention that is *unwanted* or not agreed to by both parties. It can include: sexual looks, pinching, touching, gesturing, or any other unwanted body contact. It also includes verbal comments, jokes, pressure for sexual activity or dates, sexual pictures or objects in the workplace, and attempted rape and rape. Victims are usually female and harassers male, although there are sometimes cases of females harassing males or people harassing others of the same sex.

2. Why is sexual harassment a problem? Some studies say that up to 80% of women workers have felt some kind of sexual harassment and that over 50% of women have been denied raises or promotions because they refused the sexual advances of their bosses. For the worker, sexual harassment can mean nervousness, fear, and stress; often women quit their jobs because of harassment. For the employer, harassment can mean higher turnover, more sick time, and lower productivity. For all of these reasons, the EEOC has made sexual harassment illegal.

3. Who is legally responsible if there is sexual harassment in the workplace? The employer is responsible for protecting workers against harassment. This means that the employer must be sure that there is no harassment by supervisors, co-workers, and non-employees. If a supervisor sexually harasses a worker, the employer is responsible (even if the worker did not complain to management). A worker who is fired, transferred, denied a raise, or demoted can sue the supervisor and the employer. Employers are required by law to take action against workers who sexually harass other workers as soon as the employer knows about the harassment. Where there is a union, the union must handle complaints of sexual harassment by management as it would any other grievance.

ACTION ACTIVITIES

A. COMPETENCY: Responding to sexual harassment

BRAINSTORM: Read each story and make a quick list of all the things the worker could do about the harassment.

1. Clair's boss puts his hand on her shoulder every time he comes to look at her work. He leans closely over her and sometimes squeezes her waist. She is upset about it, but is afraid she will lose her job if she says anything.
2. Manya is the only woman on a construction crew. Several of her co-workers have told her they will let her have the easy jobs if she goes out with them after work. She doesn't want to but is afraid she'll get the worst jobs if she doesn't. She is afraid they'll make her life miserable if she tells her supervisor. She is in a union.
3. Irene works in a small area with two men. They tell dirty jokes a lot and have pictures of naked women on the wall. This embarrasses her and she has told them how she feels, but they say it's a free country and they're not hurting her so she should leave them alone.
4. Anna has a problem with added work on her job. Her union representative told her he will file a grievance for her. He asked her to go for a drink after work to talk about it. She wants to talk about it at work. He hasn't mentioned the grievance since then.
5. Lee's supervisor has asked her out many times. She does not want to go out with him. He just told her that he is thinking about giving her a promotion. She is a single mother with two small children and needs the money. She is afraid that he won't promote her if she refuses him.
6. Frank works with two other men. They make sexual jokes all the time. He feels embarrassed. He doesn't want to join the joking but is afraid they'll make fun of him if he doesn't.
7. OTHER: Add a situation that you know about.

POSSIBLE RESPONSES TO SEXUAL HARASSMENT: Compare your list
to this one. What is the same or different in the lists? Add to this list:

1. Do nothing. Ignore the harassment.
2. Quit and find another job.
3. Talk to the harasser yourself.
4. Talk to other workers for support and advice; ask if they have been harassed too.
5. Keep records of times, dates, and places of harassment and what was said or done.
6. Write a letter to the harasser and keep a copy.
7. Tell your supervisor.
8. Complain to a higher level of management.
9. Get help from the union; file a grievance.
10. File a complaint with the EEOC or state agency.
11. File a lawsuit.

CHOOSING RESPONSES: Every case of sexual harassment is different.
Choosing a response depends on many things:

1. Who is the harasser? Is it a co-worker or supervisor?
2. Why is he harassing you? Is he someone you can talk to? What do you think he'll do if you talk to him?
3. How serious is the problem?
4. What will happen if you do nothing about the problem?
5. Are you in a union?
6. Have other people also been harassed?

Answer these questions for some of the stories on page 144 (you can add information if necessary). Then suggest three possible responses. Discuss what might happen for each response. Choose the best one and explain why.

B. COMPETENCY: Talking to a harasser

If the harasser is a co-worker, telling him what is bothering you is often
a good first step. It may help to have a friend or union representative with you.
The harasser may not know how you feel or what you will do to stop the
harassment. It is important to be very clear and specific about the behavior
that bothers you: you can *describe what the person is doing, how you feel
about it,* and *what change you want.*

> Example: When you whistle at me, it bothers me and I wish you
> would stop.

If the person refuses to change, you can tell him what you will do next.

> Example: If you don't stop, I will report you to the union.

Act out what you would say for each of the stories on page 144.

C. COMPETENCY: Keeping records of harassment

What are the differences between the way these two records of harassment are written?

Example #1: My foreman wants to go out with me. I said no but he keeps asking me. He touches me a lot and stands near me. He says he won't move me to a new job if I say no.

Example #2:

Jan. 12: Joe asked me out when I was on break. I said no. I told him I am married. He winked at me.

Jan. 15: I told Joe I want to move to repair. He said he could arrange it. Then he asked me out again. I said no.

Jan. 16: Joe asked me if I still want the repair job. I said yes. He said he would help me if I go out with him.

When you make a complaint about harassment, it helps to have written records of what happened. The record should be as impersonal as possible; write down what anyone would see looking at the situation. Be sure to include:

1. The date.
2. The place.
3. What the harasser said or did.
4. What you said or did.
5. Witnesses (people who saw or heard the harassment).

You should also keep anything (notes, letters) that the harasser gives you. If you write the harasser a letter, keep a copy of it.

EXERCISE: Make up records for two of the stories on page 144.

LETTER: Write a letter to one of the harassers in the stories on page 144. Be very specific about what he does that you don't like. Include dates, places, and what happened. Tell the harasser what you want him to do or stop doing.

STUDENT ACTION RESEARCH

Is there someone at your workplace who is bothering you? With the class, discuss the situation: Is it harassment? If so, plan what you might say or write a letter to the person. Report what happens; decide what to do next.

Participating in a Union

Lesson 1 Belonging to a Union

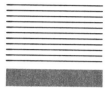

CODE

Carla: Congratulations! You're in the union now!

Marta: Big deal! Now my check is smaller. They take out two hours a month for union dues!

Carla: It's worth it. Now you get benefits. You get vacation time, sick days, and insurance. And you're protected! If you have a problem, the union will help you. You can't be fired as easily.

Marta: But they can still lay me off.

Carla: They have to go by seniority in layoffs. It's all in the contract.

Marta: That's nice. But I can't read the contract. It's only in English.

Questions for discussion:

1. What is a union? What are union dues?
  What happened to Marta?
  How does she feel about being in the union?
  How does Carla feel about the union?
  Can Marta read the contract?

2. What *benefits* does Carla talk about?
  What *protections* does Carla talk about?
  What problems and questions does Marta talk about?

3. Are there unions in your country? What are they like?
  Have you ever been in a union? If so, did it help you?
  Have you ever had problems with a union?
  Do you ever talk to your union representative or go to union meetings?
  Is union information translated into your language?

4. What benefits do workers get from unions?
  What protections do workers get from unions?
  What problems are there with unions?
  Do you think unions are helpful for foreign workers?

5. What can you do if you have a problem with your union?
  What can you do if you don't know your rights at work?
  What can you do if you don't understand union information?

THINKING ACTIVITIES

A. VOCABULARY

Discuss these words and phrases. Then match them with their meanings.

a. union dues   **I.** organizing drive
b. contract   **j.** grievance
c. local contract   **k.** seniority
d. national contract   **l.** shop steward/committeeman
e. organized shop   **m.** job action
f. unorganized shop   **n.** strike/labor dispute
g. open shop   **o.** contract violation
h. closed shop   **p.** wildcat strike

____ **1.** An agreement between the union and management about wages, working conditions, hours, job security, etc.
____ **2.** Workers or management do something against the contract.
____ **3.** Workers stop working because their contract has not been settled or there is a major job problem.
____ **4.** The amount of money you pay each month for union protection and services.
____ **5.** A workplace with a union.
____ **6.** A workplace with no union.
____ **7.** A unionized workplace where workers can choose not to join the union. The union still represents them.
____ **8.** A workplace where you must join a union or pay dues.
____ **9.** Workers or a union try to get a union into an unorganized workplace.
____ **10.** A union representative who helps workers with problems.
____ **11.** A complaint that a worker files with a union representative about a contract violation.
____ **12.** When workers do something together to complain about a problem: for example, walk-offs or sick-outs.
____ **13.** An agreement between a company and workers in all its workplaces around the country.
____ **14.** An agreement that covers conditions and jobs at one workplace only.
____ **15.** How long a worker has worked for an employer.
____ **16.** Workers walk off the job without the OK of the union.

B. EVALUATING UNIONS

Have you ever worked in a union job? Have you ever worked in a non-union job? What were some of the differences?

	Union	Non-union
pay	_____	_____
job security	_____	_____
benefits	_____	_____
problems with management	_____	_____

	Union	Non-union
hours/overtime	_____	_____
health and safety	_____	_____
discrimination	_____	_____
other _____	_____	_____

C. COMPARING UNIONS

Were you a union member in your country? Are you a union member in the U.S.? If so, compare the two unions. Which union did you like better? Why? What are some problems with the weaker union? What did the stronger union do? Now make a chart comparing unions you have belonged to.

Stronger unions	Weaker unions
_____	_____
_____	_____

D. ADVANTAGES AND DISADVANTAGES OF UNIONS

Make a class chart of some good and bad things about unions in the U.S. Start by listing Carla and Marta's ideas.

Advantages	Disadvantages
_____	_____
_____	_____

ACTION ACTIVITIES

A. COMPETENCY: Getting a copy of the contract

If you are in a union, discuss these questions:

1. Do you think it is important to have a copy of the contract? Why or why not?
2. Have you ever seen your contract? Do you have it?
3. Have you ever tried to get one? What happened?
4. Why do workers often not have their contracts?
5. What would happen if you tried to get a copy of your contract? Who would you ask? What would you say?

Add to these ways of asking for the contract.

Asking for the contract

Excuse me. I never got a copy of the contract.
I was wondering if I could have a copy of the contract?

Possible responses

Sure. But you probably won't be able to read it.
What do you want it for?
They're out of print.

Explaining your reason

I want to learn how to read it.
I want to look something up.

ROLE PLAY: Act out these conversations between union members and representatives.

1. You ask for a contract. The steward says there are none left but you can borrow his.
2. You ask for a contract. The steward says you don't need one; you can talk to her if you have problems. You insist that you want your own copy.

B. COMPETENCY: Finding out about the contract

When a contract is signed, the employer must sit down with union representatives to discuss the issues. Wages, hours, work rules, and conditions cannot be set by the employer alone. The union and the employer must agree before writing the contract. If they can't agree, there may be a strike. Add to these lists of questions that contracts often answer. If you're in a union, answer them for your workplace; if you don't know the answers, interview a co-worker. If you're not in a union, interview someone who is.

Hours
How many hours do workers have to work?
Do they have to work overtime?
How are shifts assigned?

Wages
How much will each job pay?
How do workers get raises? How much are they?

Benefits
How much sick time is there? Is it paid?
How much vacation time is there? Is it paid?
Which holidays do workers get? Are they paid?
Is there insurance? Who pays for it?

Seniority/Job security
How do you get seniority?
When does the employer have to follow seniority (layoffs/promotions/
 callbacks)?

Job classifications and promotions
How do you change jobs or departments?
How do you get promotions?

Safety and working conditions
What are the rules about safety equipment?
How are safety problems handled?
How many breaks do you have? How long are they?
How long is lunch?

Grievances
What do you do about a problem or complaint?
What are the steps in the grievance procedure?

STUDENT ACTION RESEARCH

1. YOUR CONTRACT: Try to get a copy of your union contract or another
 contract.

   a. Find four items that you understand. What pages are they on?
   b. Find four items in the contract that you do not understand. How will
    you find out what they mean?
   c. List four benefits the contract gives you.
   d. List four ways the contract protects you.
   e. Think of four things that are not in the contract that you would like
    to see in a future contract.

2. Find out what Right to Work Laws mean. Does your state have a Right
 to Work Law? Is your shop an open or a closed shop?
3. Think of one problem you had at work or one question you have about
 your rights. How will you look it up in the contract? Whom can you ask
 for help? What will you say? Read about your question or problem in
 the contract. Discuss it with class members, co-workers, and others.

Lesson 2 Participating in the Union

CODE

David: Can you help me? The boss added some work on my job.

Steward: That's because you always do everything he says.

David: But it's too much now. Could you talk to him for me?

Steward: You want me to help you but you never help anyone else. When Jose was fired last month, you didn't sign the petition for him.

David: I couldn't. I need this job. And no one told me about the petition. You never explain anything to me.

Steward: You never ask. You don't go to union meetings.

David: You take my dues but never do anything for me.

Steward: All you care about is your own job. We'll never get anything unless we stick together.

Questions for discussion:

1. What is David's problem? Why does he ask for help?
Who is the steward? Does the steward want to help him?
What happened last month?
What did David do? Why?

2. What are David's complaints about the union?
What are the steward's complaints about David?
Why doesn't David participate in union activities?

3. Have you ever asked the union for help? What happened?
Do you participate in union activities, elections, or meetings?
Have you ever had any problems with your union representative?
  What happened?

4. What are some reasons immigrants might not be active in unions?
What are some reasons a union might not help a worker?

5. What can the union do for you? What can you do for the union?
What can you do if your steward doesn't want to help you?
How can you solve problems with your union?

THINKING ACTIVITIES

A. WHAT CAN YOU DO FOR THE UNION?

People sometimes say, "The union is only as strong as its members." What do you think this means? Do you think your union wants you to participate more?

What would you say to each of these workers?

1. I have too much to do. I don't have time for the union.
2. The union never does anything for me. Why should I go to union meetings?
3. I don't understand anything anyway. The union never translates anything into my language or explains things.
4. The union people don't listen to me because my English isn't good.
5. The union doesn't care about us. It's a company union.
6. Why should I vote in the union election? The officers don't even know me.
7. (Add your own.) _____

B. WHAT CAN THE UNION DO FOR YOU?

When should you ask the union for help? Do you think you should usually try to talk to your boss about problems before you talk to the union? Why or why not?

Sometimes, you cannot solve a problem by talking to management. Your union must represent you if you are a member (even if you don't pay dues). *If your employer takes formal disciplinary action against you, you should always ask for your union representative.* The union will meet with you and management to try to solve the problem.

LEGAL INFORMATION: You have the right to union representation at any meeting with management if you think the meeting may lead to discipline, criticism, or other bad results for you.

Look at each of these situations. Write *yes* if you have the right to union representation. Write *no* if you don't.

Your boss asks to meet with you because:

_____ **1.** You have been absent a lot. Your boss wants to give you a warning.
_____ **2.** Your boss wants to explain a new procedure to you.
_____ **3.** Your boss wants to change you to a lower job classification.
_____ **4.** Your boss wants to ask you to switch to another shift but you don't want to change.
_____ **5.** You have not been doing the extra work added to your job.

You want to meet with your boss because:

_____ **6.** You have been denied a day off. You want to complain.
_____ **7.** You have a suggestion for a better procedure.
_____ **8.** You want to request a leave of absence.
_____ **9.** You reported a safety problem but it was not fixed.
_____ **10.** (Add your own.) _____

ACTION ACTIVITIES

A. COMPETENCY: Requesting union representation

If your supervisor wants to talk to you about a problem with your work, you don't have to talk to him or her until your union representative is there. Sometimes you may not know your rights in a situation. Your boss may ask you to do something that you're not sure you have to do. It's a good idea to ask your union representative about your rights.

Add to this list of ways to request union representation:

I'd like to see my committeeman.
Please put in a call for me.

Act out endings to these conversations:

1. Mr. Smith: Paul, what's the problem? You've made too many mistakes today.

Paul: There's something wrong with my machine.

Mr. Smith: Well, it still works. I'm putting you on notice. Any more mistakes and you can go home.

2. Georgia: Mr. Smith, these fumes are really bothering me. I'm having a hard time working.

Mr. Smith: I can't even smell them. Don't worry about them.

3. Mr. Smith: Anna, I want you to take over Alice's job. You're the only one that knows it.

Anna: Will I get pool pay?*

Mr. Smith: No, it's just for a week.

4. (Add your own.)

B. COMPETENCY: Requesting translations of union materials

Write down two things you could say if you or others can't read union materials. Compare your answers.

Example: There are so many Spanish workers here. We would like to know what's happening. Do you think the union could translate the newsletter into Spanish?

DISCUSSION: What would happen if you asked for a translation of union materials at your workplace? Why would it help the union? Who would you talk to about this request? What responses do you think you would get?

C. COMPETENCY: Stating opinions about union matters

Why is it important to let your union representatives know what you want or think?

Add to these ways of stating your opinion:

I think we need longer breaks.
I think we should write a petition instead.
Why don't we have a translator at the meeting?

*Pay for doing someone else's job when they're out

ROLE PLAY: Write down three important problems at your workplace.
How could the union help with these? How would you state your opinion
about this problem to a union representative or at a union meeting? In pairs,
work out conversations and present them to the class.

STUDENT ACTION RESEARCH

LOG: Think of a time when your employer wanted you to do one thing
but the union or other workers wanted you to do another (like Chung Chi's
story on page 68.) Answer these questions and write about it in your log.

What was the problem?
What did the employer want you to do?
How did you feel?
How did you decide what to do?
Who did you talk to?
Did you do what the union wanted or what the employer wanted?
What happened after you made your decision?
Do you think you made the right decision?

UNION MEETINGS: Add to this list of things that would help you understand
union meetings:

1. Go with a friend whose English is better.
2. Find out before the meeting what they will talk about.
3. Don't try to understand everything.
4. _____
5. _____

Go to a union meeting. Report back about two or three things you understood.
Report back about what was difficult. What did you like about the meeting?
What didn't you like? What could you do next time you go?

INTERVIEWS: Interview a union representative or an American worker.
Find out about the union's point of view about immigrant workers. What
problems does the union see with immigrant workers? What should
immigrant workers do to become more active? Report back to class.

Lesson 3   Organizing for Change

CODE

Notice: Little's Department Store is currently accepting applications for immediate permanent full-time and part-time employment in all Little's stores and distribution facilities. Apply in the Personnel department of your nearest Little's store or distribution facility. Little's is an equal opportunity employer.

Labor Dispute Exists

L I T T L E ' S

Questions for discussion:

1. What is this ad for?
What is happening at Little's?
What is a *labor dispute*?

2. Why is Little's advertising for workers?
How will Little's workers feel about people hired during the strike?
How will the new workers feel?

3. Have you ever been in a strike? What happened?
Have you ever been in any other action against your boss?
Have you ever refused to go on strike?
Have you ever worked somewhere where other workers were on strike?

4. Why do workers sometimes go on strike?
What is the purpose of stopping work?
Why do people sometimes apply for jobs at places where there is a strike?
How do striking workers feel about them? Why?

5. If you needed a job, would you answer this ad? Why or why not?
What can you do if your union calls a strike?
What can you do if you don't understand the reason for a strike or job action?
What can you do if you disagree with the reason for a strike or job action?
How are you protected if you go on strike? How are you protected if you don't go on strike?

THINKING ACTIVITIES

A. VOCABULARY

Match these words with the situations below:

a. job action   **b.** strike   **c.** union organizing drive

____ **1.** Union members stop work because they have no contract or because they are having a major work problem.
____ **2.** Workers decide to get a union to represent them or a union tries to get into a workplace.
____ **3.** Workers leave their jobs, work slowly, or do something else against their employer to protest a work problem.

B. JOB ACTIONS

There are five Haitian workers on one line in an electronics shop. One day, an American worker is fired. The other workers are angry. They are talking quietly to each other. No one talks to the Haitians. Before lunch, the Americans walk off their jobs with their coats. What should the Haitians do?

Before you choose a solution think about what will result from each choice. Answer these questions:

1. What does the employer want?
2. What do the union or other workers want?
3. What will happen if the Haitians do nothing?
4. What will happen if the Haitians walk off?
5. If you were working there, what would you do?
6. What are your rights?

Possible solutions:

1. They should do nothing and keep working.
2. They should walk out with the Americans.
3. Each Haitian should decide what to do by himself or herself.
4. They should ask an American what is happening and then decide together what to do.
5. (Add your own.) _____

Rank the choices from best to worst. Discuss your choices in small groups and choose a group solution.

C. STRIKES

FOR-AND-AGAINST CHART: What are the problems with striking? What are the reasons for striking? Make a chart with reasons workers might want to strike and reasons against striking.

For	Against
higher wages	no pay during strike
_____	_____
_____	_____
_____	_____

In New York City there was a major hotel strike a few years ago. During the strike, the management of several of the hotels went into ESL classes and offered jobs to the students.

1. Why did the hotels go to ESL classes?
2. Why did they think that ESL students might take the jobs?
3. What would you do in this situation?
4. Do you know any other times when immigrants took jobs during strikes? What happened?

" All they think about is money..."

READING: Legal information on the rights of strikers

Divide into groups and read about strikers' rights. Each group should read one question and report on it to the class.

1. What laws cover strikes? The National Labor Relations Act (NLRA) covers who can strike, how strikers are protected, how they can get their jobs back, and what they can do during strikes. There are also state laws about strikes. Even if you win a strike, it may take a long time to get your job back.

2. Who can strike? Workers who work for private employers can strike. In many states, public employees cannot strike (although they often do).

3. What can strikers do in picket lines? A picket line is a group of workers with signs or leaflets about their strike. You can picket on public property, but not usually on private property. Picketers can talk to or shout at people entering a workplace. They cannot touch or hurt people. They cannot stop cars or trucks trying to go to the workplace.

4. What benefits can strikers get? Often unions give workers a small amount of "strike pay." Companies can stop paying medical insurance during strikes (workers are often still covered during the first weeks of a strike). People on disability can still collect disability pay (but they should not picket). Each state has its own laws about collecting unemployment during a strike.

5. Can strikers get their jobs back after a strike? If no one was hired in your place, you have the right to return to your job after a strike. If someone replaced you, your rights depend on the reason for the strike. Workers who went on strike because of an employer's unfair labor practice can get their jobs back. Workers who went on strike for more money or benefits may not get their jobs back for a long time.

6. If union members work during a strike, can the union fine them? Yes. The union must give workers a hearing, but it can fine them or kick them out of the union.

Now look at your *For* and *Against* lists on page 157. Do you want to make any changes?

D. ORGANIZING DRIVES

When problems at work cannot be solved by one person or a small group, workers may decide to organize a union. To do this, they need to choose which union they want to represent them. The union will have an organizing drive and ask workers to sign union cards. If most workers sign, there will be an election. Read this story and give your opinions.

Maria worked in a new hotel. The pay wasn't bad, but they moved the managers around a lot. Everytime there was a new manager, he wanted to show he was the best, so he would add to Maria's workload. The workers realized that there was nothing they could do about this problem and other problems without a union. So when the Hotel and Restaurant Workers' Union started an organizing drive in the hotel, many of the workers were glad. One of Maria's friends asked her to sign a union card. Another friend told her she could lose her job if she signed. Maria liked the idea of the union, but didn't know if this was a good union. She wondered if she would lose her job. She did not know what she would get if the union won. What should Maria do?

1. Nothing. She should let the other workers decide.
2. She should refuse to sign the card. It is too dangerous.
3. She should sign the card. A union is always good.
4. She should ask questions. She should find out her rights. She should find out what the union will do. She should tell the union what she wants. She should talk to friends.

READING: Legal information about organizing drives

The NLRA says that most workers in private businesses have the right to organize for specific workplace improvements or to get a union. Public employees have the same right in most states. Employers can argue against a union but it is illegal to try to scare, punish, or bribe workers to get them to vote against the union.

Listen as your teacher reads these sentences. Put up one finger if the sentence talks about something that workers can do; put up two fingers if the sentence talks about something that employers cannot do.

1. Workers cannot be punished for complaining about conditions.
2. Workers have the right to complain to management about working conditions.
3. Workers can protest the firing, transfer, or discipline of co-workers.
4. Employers cannot punish workers for talking about a union.
5. Employers cannot promise workers higher pay, promotions, or better conditions in exchange for voting against the union.
6. Workers have the right to sign leaflets, union cards, and petitions.
7. Employers aren't supposed to say the company will close if the union wins.
8. Employers aren't supposed to tell workers they will be fired if they sign a union card.
9. Employers cannot move union supporters to worse jobs.

ACTION ACTIVITY

COMPETENCY: Getting information about job actions

Often immigrant workers are not told about union activities. You need information to decide what to do if there is a strike, a job action, or an organizing drive. Here are some ways to ask for information. Pair the phrases on the left with the questions on the right. Notice the word order in the questions:

Requests for information	Questions
I'd like to know	why everyone is leaving.
Could you tell me	what is going on.
Could you explain	what you want in the contract.
We were wondering	the reasons for calling a strike
(Add your own.)	(Add your own.)

ROLE PLAY: Act out each of these situations with *two* different endings. Discuss the differences: what would be the consequences of each choice?

1. The Haitian workers (page 157) decide to ask about the reasons for the walk-out. They want to know why the others are leaving and what will happen to them. An American worker tries to convince them to walk off, too. What do they decide to do?
2. Maria (page 159) wants more information about the union and what will happen if she signs the union card. She asks the union organizer what the union will do if it wins the election. Does she decide to sign the card?
3. There are two unions trying to organize the same workplace. Ask questions of each union organizer to find out which union to support. Some questions are: What will you ask for in a contract? Will you translate union materials? Add your own questions. Which union will you choose?
4. Have you ever worked somewhere where there was a strike, job action, or organizing drive? What information did you want? Act out the conversation with your questions.

READING: Immigrants organize

Before you read this article, look at the title. What do you think the article is about? Make up questions using *who, when, where, why,* and *how.*

After reading the article, divide into five groups. Each group should make up one set of questions for the class.

Set #1: Make questions starting with *who, where, what,* and *when.*
Set #2: Make questions with *how, how long,* and *what problems.*
Set #3: Make questions with *do you, did you ever,* and *in your country.*
Set #4: Make questions with *why.*
Set #5: Make questions with *what could, what should,* and *what would.*

The Talk Is Union, the Tongues Are Asian

by Lynda Gorov

The chattering is nonstop, animated and in Khmer, the native tongue of the three Cambodian refugees. Only one English word is uttered and the women workers use it repeatedly and heatedly: Union.

There are no unions in Cambodia and there is no equivalent for the word in Khmer, no phrase that adequately expresses the concept of collective bargaining muscle. But in the past nine months the women have become intimately acquainted with the word and have embraced the concept behind it.

The women, all in the United States less than four years, work at New England Shrimp Co. in Malden. Since August they and many other workers have been trying to form a union at the company, where nearly 70 percent of the 200 employees are Southeast Asian immigrants. Their efforts so far have been stymied at every turn and, through an interpreter whose English is imperfect, the women say their belief in America as the land of choice is fading.

"We like America, but not our jobs," says one of the Cambodians, who like the others fears company retribution and so asks not to be identified. "If the union not win, we look for new jobs. We not want to work here."

Union organizing is tough under the best of circumstances. But when the company is willing to spend money to fight the organizing effort and the employees speak little or no English, it becomes almost impossible. Local 592 of the United Food & Commercial Workers union has been trying to organize New England Shrimp workers since August. Now, some workers are as angry at the union as they are at the company.

What spurred the workers to want a union seems to have less to do with paychecks than with intangibles. The workers equate a union with having a voice on the plant floor and in the upstairs offices, where computer terminals hum. A union, they say, would mean better hours, better benefits and better treatment.

New England Shrimp's Commercial Street plant is clean and streamlined, but the workers say supervisors yell at them constantly to move faster and work harder. It is not uncommon to work 60 hours a week and while the three women workers say they enjoy earning time-and-a-half after 40 hours, they say they feel pressured to work more. Their breaks are 15 minutes in the morning and half an hour for lunch. Vacation time is minimal; paid sick days are nonexistent.

But John E. Bradley, general counsel for New England Shrimp, says the company is a decent place to work and is good to its employees. The money is good, with average earnings of $6.33 an hour, which rises to $8.45 if benefits are included. The typical worker, he says, puts in 48 to 50 hours a week, with the longest days coming during the busy winter holiday season. Production is monitored by the US Food & Drug Administration and the US Department of Agriculture. . . .

On Friday the plant and maintenance workers are scheduled to vote whether to join the union. An earlier election, called for Nov. 2, was canceled by the National Labor Relations Board (NLRB) only 30 minutes before the vote. The board's regional office in Boston had approved the election, but New England Shrimp requested a review and the NLRB in Washington ruled in the company's favor. New England Shrimp is contesting the upcoming election, too. . . .

The Washington ruling stemmed from the way the union tried to overcome what it considers the biggest barrier to organizing the plant—the language barrier. When the union wants to address the Cambodian, Laotian and Vietnamese workers, it must use an interpreter. Though the workers come from three countries, they speak five languages among them and many different dialects.

The union has never hired a professional interpreter, preferring instead to recruit the workers' spouses and neighbors to translate. The union has also relied on the workers' children, who attend local schools.

The language problems have led to criticism of the union by some who feel it has not adequately explained what a union will mean for the workers and what union dues are all about. Cambodian Ratha Yem, who helps settle refugees, says the union has spent too much time highlighting holidays and too little time talking about what unions are for and why they exist. Many workers, unfamiliar with unions and confused about this union's promises, have sought his counsel, he says. . . .

All this legal activity has taken up a great deal of time, which often is a union organizer's enemy. "The labor board is helping to break the union and keep us out of the company," says union organizer Jeffrey A. Bollen. "It's as though every time the company says it can't get something on us, the board gives them more time."

Koutsis says New England Shrimp has taken advantage of the delays by firing several workers active in the organizing drive. Kingston, the company attorney, maintains turnover is always high and that no more workers than usual have been dismissed.

"The boss say union no good, union only want your money," says one of the Cambodian workers. "They say if you go for union, you don't have job. We got to win."

U N I T IX

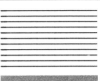

Looking Ahead

Lesson 1   Working with Americans:
All in the Same Boat

" You've done such an outstanding
job operating two machines we are
having you work a third..."

CODE

Mary: There's Chu-Li, working through her break again.

Susan: I feel sorry for her. She's killing herself and they still pay her less than we get.

Mary: She makes me mad. She's just thinking about herself. She's hurting herself and hurting us. That's why they hire immigrants. They can get more work out of them and pay them less.

Anna: Why don't you take a break, Chu-Li?

Chu-Li: I can't. I need this job.

Anna: But nobody else works that hard.

Chu-Li: But I have to make a living. I want to show the boss I'm a good worker.

Anna: What about the rest of us? We're all in the same boat here. We need to work together.

Questions for discussion:

1. What is Chu-Li doing?
Does she work more than other workers?
Does she get paid more?

2. Why does Chu-Li work through her break?
How do Mary and Susan feel about Chu-Li? Why?
How does Chu-Li feel about the other workers?
How do you think Chu-Li's boss feels?

3. Do you ever work harder than others? Why? What will happen if you work harder than other workers?
How do other workers act if you work harder?
Have you ever had a disagreement with an American about work? What happened?

4. Why do immigrants sometimes feel that they have to work harder than Americans?
How do Americans feel when immigrants work more? Why?
What do you think is a good worker? Do you think all the workers are "in the same boat"? Why or why not?
Who does it help if workers fight with each other? Who does it hurt?

5. What can workers do if their attitudes about something are different?

THINKING ACTIVITIES

A. COMPARING ATTITUDES

In order to get along with other workers, it's important to understand why *you* act or think the way you do, and why *they* act or think the way they do. Add to this list of things that people sometimes say about Americans.

1. They aren't friendly to immigrants.
2. They don't work hard enough.
3. _____
4. _____

Now pretend you are an American. What might you say about immigrants? Add to this list of things Americans might say about immigrants:

1. Immigrants work too hard.
2. You're stupid if you don't speak English.
3. Immigrants take jobs away from Americans and cause unemployment.
4. Immigrants weaken the labor movement and lower the wages for Americans.
5. _____
6. _____

In small groups, discuss each stereotype:

1. Do you think this stereotype is true? Why or why not?
2. Why do you think people say this about Americans?
3. Why do you think people say this about immigrants?
4. What could you say to refute this view or to make someone believe it's not true?

B. SOURCES OF CONFLICT AT WORK

Look at each of these reasons for problems between workers. Give examples of each from your own experience.

1. *Racism:* Thinking you're better than someone else because of your color or your nationality.
2. *Cultural differences:* Not understanding different ideas or ways of doing things; wanting to keep your own culture.
3. *Lack of previous contact:* Being afraid or embarrassed to talk to someone who is different because you've never known anyone like him or her before.
4. *History:* Disliking someone because your countries have been enemies.
5. *Economic fears:* For Americans, being afraid someone else will take your place; for immigrants, wanting to get ahead or make it.

Now read these quotes and discuss possible reasons for the problem. What does the American think? Why? What does the immigrant think? Why? Explain your answers.

1. "I'm always polite at work. I do my job and I say good morning to the other workers. But they're not friendly. They ignore me and stay away from me. I don't know what I'm doing wrong."
Possible reasons: *lack of previous contact, racism* _____

2. "If you work, Americans say you're taking a job away from someone else. If you don't work they say you're a welfare cheat."
Possible reasons: _____

3. "Sometimes Americans think they should get the better jobs because it is 'their' country."
Possible reasons: _____

4. "My partner always tells me to slow down and not work so fast."

Possible reasons: _____

5. "Whenever I try to say anything, they laugh at me and say I'm stupid because I don't speak English."

Possible reasons: _____

6. "I told the supervisor that another worker was taking extra breaks. Now no one will talk to me."

Possible reasons: _____

7. "I can't stand watching those immigrants eat; they eat with their fingers and their food smells. I'm not eating in the cafeteria anymore."

Possible reasons: _____

8. "You can't trust anyone. That Chu Li goes right to the boss if there's a problem. That's the last time I'm telling her anything."

Possible reasons: _____

9. (Add your own.) _____

Possible reasons: _____

C. DISCUSSION

Talk about a conflict between workers from your own experience. Discuss possible reasons for the conflict.

ACTION ACTIVITIES

A. COMPETENCY: Overcoming differences

There are many ways to respond when you have a conflict with a co-worker. Which do you like best? Why?

1. You can get angry.
2. You can tell your supervisor.
3. You can say nothing and go away.
4. You can talk about the problem with co-workers.
5. You can find a problem you share and work on it together.
6. Other: _____

Act out this solution to being called stupid:

John: Here. Do my job for a minute.
Jose: Pardon?
John: You're so stupid! You don't even understand English.
Jose: Excuse me. Do you speak Portuguese?
John: Of course not.
Jose: Do you speak French?
John: NO.
Jose: How many languages do you speak?
John: One. Why?
Jose: English is my third language.

What would happen if Jose actually said this?
Do you think it's a good solution?
What else could Jose do in this situation?

Act out two possible solutions to this problem:

John: Slow down! Don't work so fast.

Maria: I have to. I need this job.

John: So do I. But if you work fast, we all have to work fast.

Maria: But I'm not an American. If I lose this job, I'm stuck. It's not so easy for us to find work.

John: That's why the boss hires foreigners. You're scared all the time. If we stick together, what can he do?

Maria: That's easy for you to say.

B. COMPETENCY: Working together

Sometimes if there is a conflict at work, you may need to ask an American to help you understand it. It's probably best to ask someone who is not part of the conflict. Add your own phrases to these lists:

State the problem

Anna tells me to work slower.
Maria always makes fun of my English.

State your attitude/opinion

I'm afraid I'll get in trouble.
It makes me feel stupid.

Ask for an explanation

Why does she care?
Why does it bother her?

Ask for advice

What do you think I should do?
What can we do?

Make up a dialogue using these phrases.

ROLE PLAY: Look at the problems on page 165. Choose a problem and act out two different solutions. Afterwards answer these questions:

1. Whom would each solution help? Whom would it hurt?
2. How would the co-worker feel? How would management feel?
3. How would you feel?

STUDENT ACTION RESEARCH

JOB ACTIONS: Ask American co-workers about what bothers them at work. What problems do they have with the employer? Do you have the same problems? In class, discuss how you could work with them to solve the problem. What could you do together? Compare different solutions: legal action, group solutions, or individual solutions. What woud be the advantages of each? Discuss your ideas with the American co-workers and try to do something together.

CODE WRITING: What is one problem you have had with American co-workers? Tell the class about the problem. Write a code about the problem and questions about the code. Act out the problem with different endings and solutions. Discuss the advantages and disadvantages of each solution.

INTERVIEW: Interview an American who works with immigrants. Ask him or her about problems with immigrants at work. What bothers other Americans about immigrant co-workers? Why do the Americans feel this way? Discuss your interviews in class.

Lesson 2 Visions for the Future: Where Are We Going?

CODE

Draw a picture of yourself at work in five years. What will you be doing? Where will you be working?

Jose: I'm sick of this place. Nothing ever changes.

Mario: Well, it sure isn't like it used to be. I've seen a lot of changes since I started here.

Jose: Like what?

Mario: We have longer breaks, better pay, and more benefits. I never thought we'd get dental insurance.

Jose: Yes, but we had to fight for every penny. And it takes too long to get anything. Besides, they own you here. I'll never make it if I stay. I'm getting out of here as soon as I can. I want to be my own boss.

Mario: That's what I said ten years ago. But don't kid yourself. It's not any easier out there. You're better off staying here and trying to make things better with the rest of us.

Jose: That's easy to say, but what can we do?

Questions for discussion:

1. What does Jose want to do?
How long has Mario worked here?
What does Mario want Jose to do?
What does Jose mean by "they own you"?
What does Jose mean by "I'll never make it . . . "?

2. Why does Jose want to leave?
What changes has Mario seen in the workplace?
Why do you think Mario is still there?

3. Have you ever felt like Jose?
Have you ever felt like Mario?
What is "making it" for you?
What do you think you'll be doing in five years?
What changes have you seen in your workplace? How did they happen?

4. How do people "make it" in America?
Do you think it's easy or hard to "make it" here? Why?

5. What can Mario and Jose do to "make things better"?
How could you "make it" if you leave your workplace?
How could you "make it" if you stay in your workplace?

THINKING ACTIVITIES

A. LIFE JOURNEYS

Continue the life journeys (from page 7) into the future. What will you be doing in five years? And in ten years? What changes would you like to see?

Now draw a lifeline showing the changes you would like to see in your workplace five years from now and ten years from now. If you all work in the same place, do this as a group.

B. INTERVIEWS

Add to this list of questions to ask each other about your lifelines. Interview each other in pairs.

1. What is your vision of your future?
2. Where would you work?
3. Who would you work with?
4. What changes would you like to see in your workplace?
5. Do you think these changes are possible in your life? In your workplace?
6. What would you have to do to make these changes happen?

C. HEROES AND HEROINES

Each class member should tell or write the story of one immigrant who you think has "made it" and who you admire; it can be a friend, someone you've heard of, or someone famous. Tell what they did, what they do now, and what they had to do to get there. Explain why you admire that person.

READINGS: Making It

1. Sang Kook Nam, 37 (an engineer), and his wife, Seon Kyung, 35 (a nurse), arrived from South Korea in 1974. Nam pumped gas for the first year, saving enough to open his own gas station, then a body shop, then a used car dealership. His wife, meanwhile, started a jewelry store. In 1979 the Nams sold their businesses and went to Los Angeles, where Nam attended dry-cleaning school and within six months made a $20,000 down payment on a store. He now has five dry-cleaning stores. "We should work harder than other Americans," Nam says. "Otherwise we cannot succeed."

2. Wai-wah Cheng, 57, came to Los Angeles from Hong Kong, where he ran a successful garment business. After seven years in the U.S., he still works in a Chinese restaurant and his wife, Nyan-ying, 52, is a seamstress. Their son Joe, 22, graduated this year from Cal Tech with a degree in physics and will work at California's Jet Propulsion Lab. "I think about what they sacrificed, and it was a lot," says Joe. "You have to give up to get."

3. Mrs. Lee, 36, works in the Chinatown Cooperative Garment Factory. It is a small factory in San Francisco which is owned and run by the workers. There is no management in the factory; the women make the decisions themselves. They manage the finances, decide their own hours and wages together; they also study English together. The manufacturers who place orders in the factory still pay very low prices so, as Mrs. Chow says, "Most of us could get more money working in other places, but who could stand the bosses over you all the time? I like it here much better . . . And we do a lot of things together. We go on picnics and see places outside of San Francisco. Do I have any complaints? Well, when any of us do we bring them up at our meetings . . ."

DISCUSSION: Answer these questions for each of the stories:

1. What did the person have to do to "make it"? How easy or hard was it?
2. How many hours a day would you have to work for this choice? How much education or money would you need?
3. Could anybody do this? Could you do this by yourself? Could you do it with other people?
4. Who would benefit from this choice? How would it affect your family? Your friends or co-workers?

After you have discussed each model for "making it," each student should talk about his/her vision of "making it." How is it the same or different from these stories?

ACTION ACTIVITIES: Planning for change

A. COMPETENCY: Planning for change

Think of three things you would like to see changed in your workplace in the next year:

Problem	Possible change
1. _____	_____
2. _____	_____
3. _____	_____

Answer these questions for each change:

1. Why is it important?
2. Who would this change help?
3. Is the change possible?
4. Who do you need to talk with first (before trying to make changes)— co-workers, your family, your friends, union representatives, a lawyer?
5. How can you make this happen? What could be done?
6. What resources do you need?
7. What will happen if you do something about this problem?

Choose one of the changes and decide what steps you can take *now* to start the change process. Discuss your problem and steps with the class. Include people you need to talk to, information you need, and some actions you can take.

B. COMPETENCY: Keep writing this book!

ADD YOUR OWN READINGS: Here are two stories about immigrants taking action for change. Read the stories following the guidelines on page 21. Then find other stories about immigrants taking action or add your own stories.

ADD YOUR OWN PROBLEM-POSING LESSONS: Look back at your Log entries from this course. Which ones would you like to use as lesson material? What other workplace issues would you like to work on in class? Use the guidelines on problem-posing on page 59 to make lessons with your teacher.

Sewing on Their Own

A Corporate Campaign Nixes Plant Closing

by Jan Gilbrecht

"We'll probably make mistakes. But everyone makes mistakes. And we'll learn," Betty Chisolm told a columnist for the Oakland *Tribune*. "I look at it as a challenge. My brain is beginning to wake up. For years I just went to work, went home and watched television. I had gone to sleep. Now we have to learn everything about running a business. Take classes, training. I don't have time for television anymore. It's great."

Chisolm was speaking as a member of the newly formed Rainbow Workers Cooperative, the first worker-owned garment shop on the West Coast. The co-op was the end result of a labor and community campaign launched against the Sierra Designs Co. in Oakland, California, in October 1984 when the company announced its intention to close down its 15-year-old manufacturing facility. The shop employed about 75 people to sew the company's line of tents, jackets, backpacks, and other outdoor gear.

Many Sierra Designs employees viewed the closure as the inevitable result of the trend towards overseas subcontracting in the garment industry. Workers had seen the signs of the shutdown coming for a number of months, as boxes of garments began arriving at the company warehouse from low-wage sewing shops in Hong Kong, Taiwan, and Mexico. Almost all the workers had friends or rela-tives who had been victims of other garment shop closures.

A number of Sierra Designs workers had firsthand knowledge of the working conditions in offshore sewing shops. In fact, many had come to the U.S. in flight from the conditions in those countries. About 50% of the seamstresses were Chinese immigrants—many had gotten a start sewing in Hong Kong sweat shops. Other employees included recent Filipina immigrants and Mexican workers from the border state of Durango. Both the Philippines and Mexico host U.S. garment manufacturers which locate in free trade zones to take advantage of low wages as well as tax breaks.

* * *

At an initial meeting in early November, Sierra Designs workers and Project members discussed the need to organize the workforce into a union to negotiate more effectively with the company and to gain some legal protection for their actions. The workers formed an independent union, the Sierra Designs Workers Union (SDWU). When 80% of the workforce had signed up and elected a negotiating committee, the new union's officers asked the company for recognition so that they could begin to bargain over the closure. Sierra Designs responded by hiring a law firm notorious for union-busting, and refusing to meet with workers or recognize their union.

The dispute over union recognition was then brought to the National Labor Relations Board, guaranteeing that the issue would drag on indefinitely. In early November, the SDWU and the Plant Closures Project began organizing a community campaign which brought a cross section of Oakland-based religious and community groups and unions into the struggle against Sierra Designs. The campaign participants immediately decided to launch a boycott of Sierra Designs products in an effort to force the company to the bargaining table.

* * *

The company's image rapidly deteriorated as management continued to stonewall all efforts by workers to discuss the closure. By the beginning of December, word leaked from one retail store manager that the boycott was costing Sierra Designs 50% of its crucial Christmas sales, a figure that was later confirmed by the company during negotiations.

The final blow to the company came when the community campaign applied pressure directly on Sierra Design's parent corporation, the CML Group.

* * *

The day before the company meeting, identical lists of terms that the workers wanted included in a settlement were placed before the Sierra De-signs president in Oakland and

CML's chairman in Boston. CML management was also informed that there would be a demonstration and press conference outside the shareholders meeting to bolster statements made by workers' representatives inside if there was no satisfactory resolution to the dispute by that evening.

The threat of disruption was enough to lend an air of urgency to the negotiations, and an initial agreement was reached by midnight. Sierra Designs workers and their Bay Area and Boston supporters spent the next day celebrating instead of demonstrating.

The agreement increased severance pay and extended health benefits to workers after the closure. But the most important part of the settlement focused on provisions for local job retention. While the campaign was not successful in convincing Sierra Designs to stay in manufacturing, workers were able to win the company's assistance in setting up a worker cooperative sewing shop that would take on some of the company's production.

* * *

The Rainbow Workers Co-op (a name inspired by the rainbow composition of the workforce), made up of 32 former Sierra Designs employees, opened for business on April 1, 1985—less than six months after the original closure announcement. Worker-members comprise a strong majority on the co-op's board of directors. Initial wage levels are comparable to what workers earned at Sierra Designs, and almost all of the co-op members were able to finance their capital investment of $1,000 from the proceeds of the sale. When the co-op opened, workers started sewing on a second contract in addition to the Sierra Designs job, and other companies have begun to solicit bids.

The hard fought campaign for the jobs of these seamstresses seems to have ended happily for all. Sierra Designs now has a reliable local contractor—and a new image as a company with a progressive attitude towards labor relations. The city of Oakland can point to a real achievement in efforts at local business retention and the development of a model that can be used to assist other small businesses. For the Plant Closures Project, the Sierra Designs campaign stands as another positive example of what can happen when workers and the community work together to fight job loss.

Cambodians Protest Job Program

50 Long Beach Refugees Want Placement to Match Skills

by Henrietta Charles
Staff writer

More than 50 Cambodian refugees marched three blocks along Long Beach Boulevard Tuesday to call attention to their dissatisfaction with local implementation of a 7-month-old, state-mandated job placement program.

Following the march, officials with the Long Beach-based National Cambodian Training Association met for 2½ hours with state officials, a session that largely failed to resolve their differences.

The meeting was held in the Long Beach offices of the Catholic Welfare Bureau, which has been contracted to do assessments and job placements statewide for refugees affected by the legislation.

During the meeting, the protesters continued waving homemade signs and chanting "We Want Jobs," "We Want Skills."

At issue are questions on whether a clause in the state legislation—mandating that jobs be found for refugees who have come to California since 1983 and are receiving public assistance—intends for those placements to be for any available work or for positions comparable to what the person was doing previously.

For example, should someone who was an auto mechanic in Cambodia be placed as a janitor or dishwasher in Long Beach?

"They are supposed to help the refugee, not beat him with a stick and say you *have* to take this job," explained association president Henry Holloway.

"This denies people their rights to do certain things, to have their own destiny."

Kessara Loth, a Cambodian refugee who has lived in Long Beach for nearly a year, helped lead Tuesday's march and has been directly affected by the job placement law.

"My background is as an auto mechanic," Loth said. "I do not want to be a janitor. I want to be retrained in auto mechanics so that I can get more experience, fix cars and get off welfare.

"Those skills will help me open a business so that I can create even more jobs."

Walter Barnes, chief of the state Office of Refugee Services, met with Holloway and later talked with the protesters but said he has not found any significant problems with the handling of refugee placements in Long Beach.

"We feel the program is being administered in accordance with the legislation," Barnes said. "Jobs are not always available in the area of their (the refugee's) previous profession," Barnes said. "So we offer them jobs that are available.

"I don't know if their (the association's) concerns can go much further with me. The remaining concerns are legal issues that will have to be dealt with through the fair hearing process."

There are an estimated 375,000 refugees living in California, representing more than 25 countries including Vietnam, Laos, Cambodia, the Soviet Union, Romania, Ethiopia and Iran, according to state officials.

An estimated 20,000 to 40,000 Cambodian refugees live in Long Beach. This is the largest concentration of Cambodian refugees in California.

Barnes said an estimated 81 percent of California's refugees receive some type of government assistance—down from the 85.4 percent of a year ago.

Further, he said California will spend an estimated $658 million on government assistance to refugees this year.

Upon referrals from local social service offices, the Catholic Welfare Bureau assesses a refugee's work history, education and language proficiency and determines whether he or she is employable or must first participate in skills and language training programs.

Once the person is referred to a placement agency, a job must be found within 90 days.

Refugees who "refuse to cooperate," even if they think a carpenter's job is more appropriate to their skills than dishwashing, can have their benefits suspended for three to six months.

Appendix

Competencies

Readings

*Legal Information

Grammar

The following represent only those grammar exercises which are specifically highlighted. Grammar is integrated through communicative exercises and can be taught through charts.